Douglas Thompson is a biographer and international journalist who was based in Los Angeles for twenty years. He has interviewed most of the world's best-known film and television stars, and is a regular contributor to major newspapers and magazines worldwide.

His biographies include *Like A Virgin: Madonna Revealed*, which was an international bestseller in 1991; *Clint Eastwood: Sexual Cowboy*; and *Pfeiffer: Beyond the Age of Innocence*, which was published in 1993.

Douglas Thompson lives with his wife and daughter in an English farmhouse near Cambridge when not 'commuting' to California.

Also by Douglas Thompson

Sharon Stone

BASIC AMBITION

Douglas Thompson

WARNER BOOKS

A *Warner* Book

First published in Great Britain in 1994
by Little, Brown and Company
This edition published in 1995 by Warner Books

Copyright © Douglas Thompson 1994

A CIP catalogue record for this book is
available from the British Library.

ISBN 0 7515 1062 9

Typeset by M Rules
Printed and bound in Great Britain by
Clays Ltd, St. Ives plc

Warner Books
A Division of
Little, Brown and Company (UK)
Brettenham House
Lancaster Place
London WC2E 7EN

Contents

For H-O-L-L-Y-W-O-O-D
with thanks for the Sharon Stones of today,
yesterday and tomorrow . . .

ACKNOWLEDGEMENTS

Sharon Stone is a phenomenon and scores of people have helped in my effort to tell her story. Most are mentioned in the following text. The more shy know who they are. Thanks to Barbara Boote of Little, Brown for her enthusiasm and support. As always, extra special thanks to literary agent Judith Chilcote for her ongoing and utter professionalism.

'*Whatever* it *is, whether you're born with it or catch it from drinking fountain water, she had it*'

– Humphrey Bogart about Ava Gardner,
title star of *The Barefoot Contessa*, released in 1954

Back to Basics

'Delectable Sharon Stone emerged from the picture
with instant stardom, rave reviews, and proprietor of
the most famous pubis aureus on the planet'
— PLAYBOY, *December 1992*

She was the nobody whom nobody wanted, who took the
role everybody turned down, but when Sharon Stone went
into action *everyone* suddenly paid attention; with hindsight,
it's small wonder.

As Michael Douglas' bisexual lover in *Basic Instinct*, she
managed 1.33 orgasms per minute in her steamy sex scenes
which called for no emotional involvement but maximum
full-frontal exposure of flesh. Her performance was the closest
that mass-market film-making had, in 1991, ever come to
pornography. As seductive serial killer Catherine Tramell, she
was an evil, homicidal bitch, the Devil. It turned male-
dominated Hollywood upside down.

Someone in Hollywood once pointed out that men put
women on a pedestal and then look up their skirts. With
Sharon Stone, Hollywood looked up her skirt and then put
her on a pedestal. Tinseltown watcher Steve Rebello suggested that Stone turned the simple act of parting her legs
into the screen's greatest special effect since Charlton Heston
parted the Red Sea in *The Ten Commandments*.

Many feminists ranted and raved, and called Stone's role
and performance offensive. Others – particularly feminist fire-
cracker Camille Paglia, who called it 'one of the great

performances by a woman in screen history' – saw it as the triumphant return of the fabulous *femme fatale*. Paglia, like the other fans, adored the turn-around in male-female control, saying: 'That interrogation scene in the police station immediately became one of the classic scenes in Hollywood cinema. There you see it all: those men around her and a fully sexual woman turns them to jelly! The men are enslaved by their own sexuality.'

The interrogation room at the San Francisco Police Department: Catherine Tramell saunters in with detectives Nick Curran (Michael Douglas) and Gus Moran (George Dzunda). In the bare room are assistant district attorney John Correli, Captain Talcott and Lieutenant Walker. The proceedings are being sound- and video-recorded.

Tramell sits down directly opposite the others. She lights a cigarette.

> 'There's no smoking in this building, Miss Tramell.'
> *Tramell confidently and coolly replies: 'What are you going to do, charge me with smoking?' She blows smoke towards Nick Curran.*
> *The interview goes ahead.*
> *Correli: 'Would you tell us the nature of your relationship with Mr Boz?'*
> *Tramell: 'I had sex with him for about a year and a half. I liked having sex with him. He wasn't afraid of experimenting. I like men like that. Men who give me pleasure. He gave me a lot of pleasure.'*
> *Correli: 'Did you ever engage in any sado-masochistic activity?'*
> *Tramell: 'Exactly what do you have in mind, Mr Correli?'*
> *Correli: 'Did you ever tie him up?'*
> *Tramell: 'No. Johnny liked to use his hands too much. I like hands and fingers.'*

Sharon Stone as her creation Catherine Tramell spreads her legs and moves ever so slightly towards Michael Douglas' Nick-Curran.

The flash. But not in the pan.

1

Sexcess

'If you have a vagina and a point of view, that's a deadly combination'

– Sharon Stone, April 1992

Sex sells. Sharon Stone is a multi-millionairess. The two facts are intimately involved. The controversial actress is the screen's sexual sensation of the 1990s and a power player in Hollywood. This is a woman who has calculated her way to the top. And her major weapon was, and is, her raunchy sex appeal. She's 'sold' herself harder and faster than any other actress in cinema history – her marketing image: the woman with the hot body and attitude to match.

There is no silly coyness about her and she admits that after a dozen years of struggling she had to do *something* to get attention: 'Time was running out and I needed to be a movie star.'

So, in 1990, she took her clothes off for *Playboy* magazine, and her long legs and wet blonde hair and all the bits in between were on display. On the cover she was bare-breasted and sucking an ice cube. She offered some philosophical thoughts to accompany the nude layout, including: 'I like a man whose brain is more expansive than his penis' and 'sex is so much more in the mind than in the body.'

Now, the centrefold wisdom from *Playboy* is normally delivered by superbly – physically – developed young ladies who have just reached twentysomething. The girls chatter on about their ambitions, their likes and dislikes, their turn-ons and turns-offs. Sharon Stone plunged into their pages at the age of thirty-two and talked sex. She didn't rattle on about skiing or her love of labradors or her ambition to be one of the human race's most helpful members.

'Lips really do it for me: big, full lips. When I was fourteen this boy told me he'd teach me how to kiss if I'd meet him in the auditorium during our free period. He sure taught me how to kiss, how to *feel* it, how to give someone room to kiss you back. I was very young and sexually immature then. I was always a great student, however.'

Yet, after an initial sprint, she was a slow starter in Hollywood. She went from the anonymity of small-town American farmgirl to New York model (in the days before the catwalk could grant super-model celebrity) to Woody Allen's fantasy girl in *Stardust Memories* in 1980.

Allen, no slouch with the ladies, decided that, from the hundreds of actresses he auditioned, Sharon Stone was the girl of most men's dreams. A decade or so later, Allen's instincts were emphatically proved correct. The intervening years were a stormy professional and domestic time for Stone.

'I was like a big mannequin – a prop in the movies I appeared in. I felt so compressed. It was excruciating. I often got really sick in the middle of production. I just couldn't face it anymore. Yet I went on because I was paying my dues, trying to be a good girl, trying to do the right thing.'

So it was absurdly ironic that playing the bad girl in *Basic Instinct* should turn her life around, make her a sex symbol on a scale with Marilyn Monroe, get her more film offers than any other actress in the world and much, much more money too.

In 1993 America's *Premiere* magazine put her at number 54 on their much watched and followed '100 Most Important People in Hollywood'. She scored way above Jane Fonda, Barbra Streisand, Goldie Hawn and many tycoons. But wasn't it just a moment ago that she was 'the blonde' – the prop, as she puts it – in a string of films which, to be charitable, were simply amiable?

Her 'overnight' success, after the world looked up her skirt in *Basic Instinct*, says a great deal about Sharon Stone's almighty drive and determination, and everything about Hollywood.

She grew up in Meadville, Pennsylvania, a small (pop: 14,258 in 1994) and quiet work-ethic type of community in the north-western borders of the steel state, directly across Lake Erie from where her future-life rival Madonna was brought up in Michigan. As a teenager, she bragged to her friends that she was going to replace Marilyn Monroe as the cinema's greatest blonde bombshell. She'd tell anyone: 'Ever since I was six, watching Fred Astaire and Ginger Rogers, I knew I was going to be an actress.'

But in 1990 she felt so low and disenchanted with her career that she was considering quitting Hollywood. She thought about studying law (her IQ at 154 is as well-endowed as her body) or teaching acting. Now, with her fame firmly established, she insists she *really* was going to sashay away from the movies.

Dutch film director Paul Verhoeven changed her plans – and her life. Verhoeven, who had established himself with the Tinseltown moneymen with the hugely successful techno-pop action movie *Robocop*, had worked with Stone on the out-of-this-world Arnold Schwarzenegger vehicle *Total Recall* in 1990. In a sense, it was Stone's breakthrough movie, with Michael Wilmington in the *Los Angeles Times* writing: 'Rachel Ticotin's brunette rebel registers less strongly than Sharon Stone's ambiguous blonde slut-wife.'

But reviews like that were no instant passport to the high-profile role of bisexual killer Catherine Tramell in *Basic Instinct*. Even then, mainstream Hollywood was asking 'Sharon who?'. Verhoeven really, really wanted Geena Davis for the role. He saw her as tall and threatening and, of course, sexual. Greta Scacchi was another contender, as were, at one time or another during pre-production, Julia Roberts, Michelle Pfeiffer, Debra Winger, Ellen Barkin and Lena Olin.

The role, the sex and violence – playing the Devil at 36-24-36 – frightened and disturbed some of the leading ladies approached. Sharon Stone saw nothing but a chance for the big time.

She went all the way for it: 'All the girls who turned down *Basic Instinct* were stupid. I wanted the part badly. When I got the role, I thought: "This is the opportunity of a lifetime. I'm either gonna play this part and rock things or hang my head in shame at the supermarket." It was an all-or-nothing roll of the dice. I believe that if you have the right equipment and a point of view that's a deadly combination,' she said. She didn't care that her 'stupid' remark might upset her peers.

And after the worldwide and continuing video success of *Basic Instinct,* she doesn't have to concern herself too much about how the leading lady competition perceives her. As she said cheerfully in the summer of 1993: 'They'd pay me to play Lassie.'

They would indeed – especially if feasibility studies and the demographics implied it was a good investment. Hollywood *needs* sex symbols and Sharon Stone is amply filling the vacuum. A Monroe cult has developed around her, but she's also got the platinum blonde Jean Harlow razzamatazz. She's forthright and cheeky, and not afraid to say what she wants or be who she is.

In Harlow's 1933 movie *Dinner At Eight*, the last lines go:

Harlow: *'You know, the other day I read a book. It said that machinery is going to take the place of every profession.'*
Co-star Marie Dressler: *'Oh, my dear, that's something you'll never have to worry about!'*

More than sixty years later, Sharon Stone could slip into that movie and dialogue without missing a beat. The difference between her and the stars of yesterday, like Harlow, Veronica Lake, Lana Turner, Betty Hutton, Jane Russell, Jayne Mansfield, Monroe and the others, is Time. She is very much a 1990s woman.

And fame arrived late. She wants the power and control that her instant icon status allows her. Her asking price for a film is now $6 million – plus percentages and perks. Her main and younger rival for roles is Julia Roberts, who has spent much of her on-screen time, most recently in 1994's film adaptation of John Grisham's *The Pelican Brief*, being rescued by men. With Sharon Stone, you feel she might be threatened by men, but never, never rescued.

She was cleverly cheated by producer Robert Evans into taking the part of the lonely, newly divorced and vulnerable New York book editor in 1993's techno-sex thriller *Sliver*. The film took a critical hammering. It had Stone's masturbation sequence in the bathtub, steamy but not convincing sex with co-star Billy Baldwin and an absurd plot with an ending – rewritten five times – which was still plain silly. But audiences wanted to see Sharon Stone.

Sliver made money. In its first weekend in America – and that was after all the reviews had been printed – it earned more than $12 million at the box-office. It made $36 million in the US and $78 million around the world – more, overseas, than Jack Nicholson and Tom Cruise's *A Few Good Men* and Clint Eastwood's action thriller *In The Line of Fire*. In December 1993, it staggered Hollywood executives by becoming the hottest video rental in America. It was in far greater demand than Sylvester Stallone's *Cliffhanger*, which had taken twice as much as *Sliver* at the box-office and marked the Rocky/Rambo star's return to form. Corporate Hollywood wisely nodded their collective heads.

Sharon Stone could, on her name alone, bring in audiences. Few actors can. This was a major star – at the cinema and the video shop. And one who was willing to work for her stardom. Sherry Lansing, the head of Paramount Studios, who made Stone's 1994 movie *Intersection*, said: 'Even after *Sliver* did not do well domestically, she travelled tirelessly around the world to support its foreign bookings. Everyone who makes a movie should do that, but Sharon is one of the few who does. Arnold Schwarzenegger does it. Michael Douglas does it. That is what makes you an international star.'

Which is what Sharon Stone is. Whenever she goes out in public it is an *event*. Once, she was an admired but anonymous model in Paris and Milan and Tokyo. Now, when she attends the Collections, she is mobbed. The word on *Basic Instinct* preceded her to the Cannes Film Festival in 1992.

'I had been there before with *Total Recall*, so I thought it might be dizzy. But it was overwhelming. I had said: "I need two bodyguards," but in fact I needed ten. I couldn't leave my hotel room without many people flanking me, pushing back hundreds of people clawing at me, grabbing me, chanting my name. It was that way wherever I went. It was very, very scary because Sharon Stone wasn't me anymore, it was *her*. And they wanted *her*. I thought: "If they're going to have her, who am I gonna have?" I really had to sit down after that and separate Sharon Stone from me, because she couldn't be me anymore. Or I would go under. So, they wanted her to be big, they wanted her to be fabulous, to say this and do that. OK, she has to be that, I made plans based on it.'

Sharon Stone was the covergirl for American *Vogue* in December 1993, and the magazine's editor Anna Wintour explained her decision: 'Sharon is a great, glamorous movie star in an old-fashioned way, when so many actresses are anti that.'

Around the same time, Stone was pushing her movie *Intersection* and, like a chameleon, turned up in what she considered appropriate guises for her interviews. And also with her preconceived conversation.

For the *New York Times* she wore horn-rimmed glasses and a see-through shirt, telling interviewer Suzanna Andrews: 'Pockets strategically placed!' She talked literature and art.

For a film magazine she struck a sizzling pose, draped across the top of a grand piano. She took her shirt off for *Vanity Fair* – she said she was conned into doing it – and was seen holding her bare breasts on the cover. And for *Rolling Stone* magazine she pondered on the sex life of ladybugs. On television she flirted with American talk-show host David Letterman, and was the perfect lady for US TV matriarch interviewer Barbara Walters. For the TV breakfast show *Good Morning America* she wore a pink bathrobe.

It is all *calculated*.

By early 1994, the danger signals were being flagged. Sharon Stone was talking about wanting to 'grow as an artist'. In *Intersection*, playing Richard Gere's wife, she was an icy, self-contained woman coping with a marriage falling apart. And, even in a love scene with Gere, she kept her clothes on. A cold role.

Joe Eszterhas, the wily and also calculating journalist-turned-screenwriter who commands $3 million an assignment, wrote the Glenn Close/Jeff Bridges courtroom drama *Jagged Edge*, *Basic Instinct* and *Sliver*. He knows Stone and Hollywood very well: 'Moving away from her star persona could be a very dangerous process. Stallone was certainly hurt when he decided to become a yuppie comedian. She should keep that in mind.'

She did. Within weeks of Eszterhas' remarks in January 1994, she was flying from Los Angeles to Miami to start work on *The Specialist*. It is a mainstream, mass-market movie packed with thrills, spills and sex. Her co-star was the reborn box-office giant Sylvester Stallone, whom she'd beaten in video sales the previous year. The casting was clever, the co-stars reflecting each other's fame and popularity: the biceps and the bombshell.

'That one is going to be in the blockbuster category,' said Stone's manager Chuck Binder. You didn't have to be biased or psychic to agree with him. On paper it was a $50-million opening weekend. Mega.

His client – since 1986 – was making all the right moves – and movies. After *Sliver* and *Intersection*, she went immediately on location in Arizona to make *The Quick and the Dead*. It was a major and strong role for her – she plays a tough and raunchy gunslinger out to avenge her father's death. The killer is played by the hugely admired Gene Hackman, who won the Oscar for Best Supporting Actor in 1993 for his role as the evil sheriff in Clint Eastwood's *Unforgiven*.

Stone is riding in classy company: *The Quick and the Dead* was regarded as an event movie for release in the autumn of 1994, there was *The Specialist* with Stallone, there were meetings about her playing Marlene Dietrich in a big budget film biography of the bisexual star. And, of course, she had contracted for a fee of $7 million to star in the sequel to *Basic Instinct*, reprising her role as the sexual and deadly Catherine Tramell. Had she slept with a woman in real life?

'I've never had sex with a woman, but I've been on dates with women. I'm not intentionally a tease. A gay woman asked me out on a date and I've gone out on a date to see if . . . 'cause, you know, men can be annoying. So once in a while you hope – Oh, God – maybe there could be an alternative.

'But unfortunately for me there isn't. I love women. I love being with girl friends. God! If I could get into it, it would be great. But, you know, it don't mean a thing if it ain't got that schwing!' she says, pushing up her hips and simulating an erection.

Sexcess?

2

Erotic Superstar

'I do think of her as a professional athlete'
– Michael Douglas, 1993

Sharon Stone's 1990s movies were called 'the acceptable face of erotica'. Video has changed the whole concept of sex and turn-on movies. In the 1970s there were the Sylvia Kristel *Emmanuelle* films (the original still sells 600 copies a month on video), in the 1980s it was *9½ Weeks* with Kim Basinger and Mickey Rourke and *Wild Orchid* with Rourke and real-life lover Carrie Otis, which tried to cash-in on the same audience.

And then Stone arrived. With *Wild Orchid*, the most talk was about whether Rourke and Otis really had sex or simulated it on camera. The same question was asked about Stone and Michael Douglas in *Basic Instinct*.

True to her fondness for shock talk and attention, Stone would confuse the astonishingly heated debate with lines like: 'Look, I have a four-minute sex scene with Michael Douglas in which I have three orgasms. What does that tell you? Michael Douglas and I went as far as anyone can go. I didn't know how they'd ever get a censorship rating.'

She is a right-between-the-eyes sex symbol, a pin-up who is not embarrassed by her sexual desires. She has made sex her currency. While most Hollywood actresses complain about the difficulty of doing nude scenes, Stone seems more comfortable in a little lingerie. Or less.

After years of 'being the blonde' – albeit a stunning one – she was exasperated: 'Once I realised that I had become a good actress, which I realised by working in my acting class, not by doing the terrible movies I was doing, I started to realise that, in order to be able to be a great actress and have access to great material, I needed to be a movie star. And I was so old that I was gonna have to do something fast to make it happen. So I did, you know, these publicity things.

'No one thought I was sexy. I kept getting back – "she's no leading lady".' Her ten pages in *Playboy* rather stopped the not-sexy argument. She was stapled to the pages wearing nothing but wisps of fantasy: 'It wasn't exactly subtle. It was like through the megaphone: "Hey, look at this!"'

'It's rare to get a working actress, who is making a living, to do that,' says her manager Chuck Binder, with a that's-my-girl cheerfulness.

Subtlety, of course, had nothing to do with the highly bankable persona she had created. Sherry Lansing, a former model and actress and independent producer – she and her partner were responsible for Michael Douglas' other controversial film, *Fatal Attraction* – who, with her job at Paramount, is now one of the most powerful women in Hollywood, says of Stone: 'She has a great sense of humour about her sex image. I saw her just after *Basic Instinct* was released, before her celebrity became so enormous, and I was very impressed. She's not afraid to be who she is. I just adore her. Not even speaking professionally – speaking as a person meeting another human being – I just liked her. There is a directness to her that I find thoroughly refreshing. I can't say that we became friends because it's not like we have lunch every week, but I had a real special empathy with her.

'I think what people respond to on-screen, other than the fact that she's a wonderful actress, is this kind of *person*. You feel a presence in the room when you're talking to her and I think that comes across on screen. There is no incredible bullshit trait to her.'

Michael Douglas is certain of her dedication: 'I do think of her as a professional athlete. She's got kind of a jock mentality and a professional athlete's discipline. I wouldn't call her inherently sexy – though she's a beautiful woman – but she certainly uses her sexuality, among her other skills, much like an athlete might use his different moves.'

Sharon Stone *is* seductive. The demographic studies they commission every five minutes in Hollywood say that men adore her and so do women. She is a marketing gem. Men want her, while women want to be like her.

She had appeared in dozens of television commercials as the Diet Coke girl, the Clairol girl, the Charlie girl and many others, seventeen films and the biggest TV mini-series ever filmed – she was Robert Mitchum's sexually wayward daughter-in-law in *War and Remembrance*, the sequel to the adaptation of Herman Wouk's *The Winds of War*, in 1988. But Stone remained a second-league player in Hollywood. This was no instant discovery of an innocent, naïve, young blonde from the backwoods or a table at Schwab's coffee shop on Sunset Boulevard.

Why, then, Sharon Stone?

A combination of luck and determination on her part, and also of Hollywood's need to keep satisfying the appetite of audiences who wanted to see cinema go further and further to the edge of what is acceptable to the mainstream.

'We talk of attention-spans all the time,' said Professor Harry Livingstone of California's Stanford University in 1994, adding: 'But it's the old joke. People want something new to replace what they've lost interest in. And they want it now! The cinema's no different from books – tastes and values change. *Lady Chatterley's Lover* would not run into problems today.

'This lady Sharon Stone simply stepped into a role which won her incredible notoriety – at this time. She and the film-makers will probably find that they have to go further and further to thrill their audiences.'

'Most actresses don't regret taking off their clothes for the screen,' said Dr Glenn Wilson, author of *Psychology of the Performing Arts and the Great Sex Divide*. He added: 'They have great bodies and are often pleased they did it when they had lovely figures rather than when they've lost them. People want to see sex and nudity. It's not harmful. There are far more harmful things. We have gone further in the horror film genre than in the sexual domain.'

Bo Derek agrees with him – to an extent. She knows much about selling sex on screen. She became a worldwide star in 1980 as Dudley Moore's much lusted-after sex object in *10*. Then she was naked in *Tarzan* and wildly seduced in *Bolero*. Talking at her ranch in California's Santa Ynez Mountains near Santa Barbara in January 1994, she laughed: 'I feel such a prude now. My films weren't sexy films. They were nothing, nothing! I never thought I would feel prudish in this business and about film projects, but I know what's coming.' Racier than *Basic Instinct* or *Sliver*? 'I've read the scripts. I'm telling you this next group of films is just unbelievable.'

Which makes you consider how far they would have to take *Basic Instinct* 2 to match audiences' expectations. Did Bo Derek think that future leading ladies, who might be required to further their careers by appearing in films which might be considered pornographic were being exploited?

'No, no. I don't feel sorry for them at all. What's there to feel sorry about? They're simulating sex in a film. I find it much worse to simulate sick violence and glamorise that. Simulated sex is nothing. I mean, it's something so impersonal. I'm sorry everybody has to make such a big deal about it, that's the thing. It's so silly.

'Actresses are going to auditions with directors now, wearing no underwear. That seems to be the latest thing. You see, they really, really want to be stars. I don't understand that kind of desperation, but I know it exists.'

Certainly, there was a desperate exasperation about Sharon Stone when she went after her landmark role in *Basic Instinct*.

Arguably it was her determination and willingness to do anything to be a star that provided the catalyst for what was to become a controversial, completely new trend in films. Coupled, if that's the word, with the movie style of Dutch-born Paul Verhoeven, who was fifty-four in 1994. He does not look like a sex freak; there's more of the university professor about him, with his soft, round face and spectacles. In Europe he established himself with films like *Soldier of Orange*, *Turkish Delight*, *Spetters* and *The Fourth Man*. Hollywood lusted after some of his talent for action and erotic movies. He gave them *Robocop* in 1987 and *Total Recall* three years later.

He had, in Michael Douglas, an established box-office star and Oscar-winner and a commitment from him about what sort of movie they wanted to make. At the Sony Studios in Hollywood, after the first international screening of *Basic Instinct* in the spring of 1992, when asked for his interpretation of the film, Douglas smiled and answered quickly: 'Sex and violence.' Did it have any redeeming values? 'No. I think it entertains you, emotionally moves you and makes you hot and scared.'

Well, there was no way of misunderstanding *his* perception of the film. But to make it work, he and Verhoeven needed an actress willing to share, in every way, their vision. Throughout her career Sharon Stone had given some gutsy, promising and established performances, but she had never had a vehicle which put her in the driver's seat and on display. How could Verhoeven be anywhere near sure that he could get the performance he needed from her?

She had the body, the icy blue eyes, the long blonde hair and the endless legs, but actresses require a certain attitude to be prepared to go all out for 'real' sex scenes without the benefit of body doubles. European actresses have often provided the requisite package: Julie Christie, Greta Scacchi, Jackie Bisset and Isabelle Adjani. In fact, Adjani was Michael Douglas' first choice as a co-star, but even this Continental was not comfortable with the nudity and sex scenes . . . And that was before Verhoeven began putting more risqué raunch into Joe Eszterhas' original screenplay.

Did Sharon Stone have the right stuff?

'I knew Sharon from *Total Recall* and she had these qualities in her already. But I, and Michael to a certain extent, had to be attracted to her in a romantic and erotic way to be able to shoot the film in an erotic way. If I did not like her personally, it would be impossible to make it work. There was a kind of attraction between Michael and Sharon too, just enough to make it work, although there were no deeper elements happening there – it was all performance. Michael told me he could see enough in Sharon's eyes to make it work.

'As the director, I was in this triangle between Michael and Sharon, and this psychological and sexual attraction is essential on set. I have a love-hate relationship with Sharon which developed on *Total Recall*. She once said: "He loves me and I hate him." That's not true. It's a relationship where we have love for each other. I had big fights with Sharon but we made up all the time, there was a lot of hugging and kissing on set.

'We push each other's buttons. There's a lot of erotic tension between us. But if you give this sexuality a chance you lose control. If you are going to consummate this "sexual" relationship with an actress, it won't work on screen anymore; it cannot end up in bed with the director!'

But Stone was having sex during filming. She says a love affair finished with the end of filming. Was it someone working on *Basic Instinct*? She's sassy and shrewd on the subject: 'I'm not prepared to reveal that. But the person will know.'

How did she get along with Michael Douglas? 'I had met him on two or three occasions before I tested with him for the movie. I really felt he and I could have a certain strange, dynamic energy together. I was never comfortable around him and I don't think he was comfortable around me. But our energy together was strong. It was a primal thing for me. It was all about watching him, observing his movements, provoking him. If one were to believe in karma, I would say there is some karmic circle yet unfilled between the two of us.'

We might suspect the American censor took a rather different view of that last remark. To get a mainstream US rating, specific scenes had to be edited from the film. Was it sex or violence? She answered: 'It was oral sex from both of us. An exchange of oral sex.'

To explain the scenes that were cut from the US version of the film, but retained in overseas versions, she used a fork and spoon to indicate her performing oral sex on Douglas: 'You see a close-up of my head here with my eyes looking up at him. Then you see him, like, between my legs. So it's definitely *us*, not body doubles. We did everything but anal intercourse and I don't know why *that* wasn't in there because, with so much violence in the characters' sexuality, that absence seems odd. Michael Douglas and I went as far as anyone could go.'

3

Young Love
and Death

'Sharon was born posing. She *came out* posing'
– Sharon Stone's mother, Dorothy, 1993

It takes a time to find Meadville, Pennsylvania, which sleeps on the American side of North America's Great Lakes. That's on a map. By plane and car, the task is much longer. Meadville is one of those tiny towns that's near everywhere but near nothing. In America, getting there somehow always involves travelling for a day. For Sharon Stone, getting *out* of town took nearly twenty years.

Growing up, she felt like a freak with her Einstein of an IQ, rated at 154. She was born in the rural community on 10 March 1958, to Dorothy and Joseph Stone, the second of their four children. (Her older, by seven years, brother Michael, who spent two years in prison for drug offences, appears in her film *The Quick and the Dead*.) She says: 'I was never a kid. I walked and talked at ten months. I started school in the second grade when I was five – a real weird, academically driven kid, not at all interested in being social. I felt out of place, I was incredibly weird, just like so incredibly weird. I was, like, forty at birth.'

Her loyal and loving mother agrees: 'Sharon has been posing from the day she arrived. She *came out* posing. I have pictures of her where she's barely able to stand, and she has her hand up behind her head.'

She was, especially in the environment of small-town America, a freak. People in Meadville get up, do their chores, go to work, come home and gossip, eat dinner and watch the nightly evening news. They complain that Walter Cronkite, the trusted grandfather of US television news, has retired from broadcasting. So how could they cope with a toddler with attitude?

Sharon Stone revealed in 1993: 'I started school and drove everybody crazy because they realised I had popped out as an adult. I had adult questions and wanted adult answers. I was a very intense, weird kid. My mother would just look at me, horrified.

'We had a very deep, revealing conversation in which she told me that she had no idea what to do with me when I was a child. I was so different from the other kids that it was frightening, scary for her. She never knew how she was supposed to treat me.

'My Dad was among those who thought I was an alien. My father was very rigid when we were young. If I was one minute late home, he was standing in the window. When I was a kid he was "that guy". Now I can call him when I have a broken heart or a mini-broken heart. But when we were young . . . since I had the ability to do things other kids didn't, he drove me towards perfection with a whip and a chair. That's very overwhelming. He's not like that now. Now, he's the sweetest guy. We've all grown . . . As a kid I didn't think I was special. I thought I was wrong. Just wrong. I never fitted in. Everything I did and said made everybody uncomfortable.

'My parents knew that I was smart. They tested me like I was a guinea pig or a hamster running on the wheel. I took endless IQ tests and put pegs in holes and matched colours with colours. I took Rorschach tests and evaluative tests about what you're predisposed to be and do. I had a high IQ and was predisposed to do technical things – science, engineering, math. I'm sure a career as a chemical engineer would have been appropriate for me, though my personality is more fitting for a lawyer.'

She says all the testing simply made her feel 'more peculiar' in a town where everything off the norm had to be avoided. At five, she was correcting her mother's grammar, and her education was a bumpy ride – literally, sometimes – from there.

'Recess was a drag until I realised I didn't have to play, that I could lean against a wall and read,' said Stone. 'At home I was a nerdy, ugly duckling who sat in the back of the closet with a flashlight and read.'

With her high IQ, the authorities of Saegertown School District dragged her through the hallways – once, physically – of education. She sped from one class to the next. She didn't learn to stop asking questions (a couple of decades later, she still hadn't) so she remained the outcast. And did what loners do. She hated school and the authority figures who bugged her, so – like so many youngsters – she created her own world. It was the beginning of the Sharon Stone phenomenon. She started wearing 'costumes' – what she would say later was an 'existentialist choice' – and staging plays in her parents' garage.

Her parents were also born in Pennsylvania, and met when they were in their mid-teens. At fifteen, they had both left school. Joe Stone went into the tool and die business. He worked the 3 p.m. to 11 p.m. shift, lifting steel blocks and cutting them up in the dark, Dickensian factory. Her mother went back to school and took evening classes and then, when her husband arrived home at nearly midnight, would sit up with him – teaching him what she had learned. Sharon Stone remembers: 'My dad kept telling me: "There's a great opportunity in engineering."'

Joe Stone, with four children to feed and educate, earned around $15 thousand a year while his family were growing up. He worked hard for others before starting his own engineering business and explained: 'My Dad died when I was four years old and, hell, I've been raised by women all my life. When I went to live with my grandmother, she was seventy-four years old, and my mother went to work in an institution, where she had to stay there at night, so she couldn't be with us.

'I tried to make things a little more comfortable for my kids. I worked in a machine shop for thirty years before I started my own business. Took a long time. Having been raised by women, I like to see women get a fair shot at life. They haven't for a long time.'

His adoring wife Dorothy, whom he calls Dot, agrees: 'I think women have to sound a little hard – or, that is, have men think they're hard. You can't be a whiner. You have to be strong or men discount everything you say.'

They were born and lived and live in little America, which has parameters of prudishness that would squeeze a naughty word, never mind a naked daughter, trying to make its way through town. Did *Basic Instinct* or their daughter's nude lay-out in *Playboy* shock them, upset them, horrify them?

'Why should it?' asks Stone's father. 'We all do it, right? It didn't embarrass me any. I thought she looked beautiful in the magazine. If it helped her career, why not? She knew that, living in such a small town, it would affect us and asked for my approval. This is her life, our lives – I gave it happily. Did it embarrass me? No. No.' Dorothy Stone is also supportive: 'It's a role and we understand it's a role. Of course, our next door neighbour might not see it in the same way we do, but we understand what's she's doing.'

But her parents didn't always understand or appreciate her antics while she was growing up. During the 'streaking' fad, their daughter would strip off and run naked around the house. Schoolfriends remember her as 'wild' and tell stories of how she nearly died twice in accidents. As her first love did.

Lou Severo went to Saegertown High School with Stone, and had several teenage dates with her. But he says her first big romance was with Craig Grindell, the only son of a rich family who owned several factories in the Meadville area. Grindell Junior drove a $35,000 Corvette sports car. Severo says of his rival for Stone's affection: 'Craig was a handsome guy from the wealthiest family in town. Sharon saw him as her ticket out of Meadville and to the big city. He was crazy, did exactly as he pleased and listened to no one, which really turned her on. But one night his luck ran out. I was with a bunch of guys drinking and drag racing on a stretch of country road. Craig was very drunk and wanted to prove his 'Vette was the fastest car in town. He was probably going more than 100 mph when his car smashed into a concrete barrier and disintegrated. His passenger was thrown more than two hundred feet, but Craig was burned beyond recognition in a huge fireball.'

Dee Dee Snedeker lived, and still lives, next door to where Stone grew up and recalls: 'She was inconsolable. She might have married him, it was the worst tragedy of her life. At the funeral Sharon was so grief-stricken she had to be supported or she'd have fallen to the ground.'

There was more tragedy in her hometown life. She took up with high-school football star Ray Butterfield and they became *the* couple on campus. Sharon Stone won't even consider talking about Butterfield today – the memory still seems too painful. But his mother Joyce, who stills lives in Meadville, revealed: 'They were very much in love. They used to ride his motorcycle all the time. She would come to the house and they'd sit for hours talking and listening to music. And when she wasn't here, they'd be on the phone for hours. They went to the prom together and Ray was killed two months later.'

Ray Butterfield's motorcycle went out of control and swerved off the road between his and Stone's home. 'We never did find out why he ran off the road. He was killed instantly,' said his mother, adding: 'I'm surprised Sharon wasn't on the bike with him the night he died. They had arranged to go out riding together earlier that day. Sharon was in total shock for weeks after the accident. She couldn't stop crying at the funeral. I held her in my arms and she sobbed: "I loved him so much." If Ray had lived I'm certain their relationship would have developed into something permanent.'

Later, Stone would escape from her own driving accident on a bitter winter day in 1974, when her Ford hit an ice patch near her home and went out of control. In the police report, witness Jimmy Tonko says: 'She was thrown from the car and narrowly missed hitting a tree with her head. That would definitely have killed her.'

Her neighbour Dee Dee Snedeker visited her in hospital and remembers: 'She was miserable with her face all puffed up black and blue. But she was a survivor and tough. You would never accuse Sharon of being a delicate girl. She kept her sense of humour and survived.'

But only just. Stone has a startling scar across her neck, which you can see in some of the steamy *Basic Instinct* sex scenes. The actress likes to recount lurid tales about the injury, that it was done by gangsters or in some sordid back-alley fight. In fact, she nearly decapitated herself riding a pony.

Her mother Dorothy still shivers at what might have been: 'She was on a pony that hadn't been ridden often and it ran under a clothesline. She passed out and fell off straightaway, otherwise it would have killed her. For a long time after she never wanted anyone to touch her neck.' Dee Dee Snedeker said: 'We thought she'd broken her neck – she got a deep, half-inch wide scar stretching across her neck.'

'All my life I covered it up,' says Stone, adding, 'I'd get up, do my morning thing and put make-up over the scar. But I've stopped doing that now. Liz Taylor has a scar, I have a scar – tough shit. I'm using it to create mystery and allure about myself. I've told a lot of great stories about it already.' Storytelling is something she does well.

Her classmates at Saegertown High School talk of her as

'cute as a button', but she puts herself down in the beauty stakes in the early years: 'I was pretty unattractive. I was tall, unbearably thin, wore thick glasses and had no sense of myself as a female. My senior year, I started to wake up to the possibilities. I looked at magazines, saw all these make-overs and thought: I can do that. I tried to dress cooler. I dyed my hair black, then brown and then red. It was like a math problem. How do you get it to equal what you want?'

'Sharon was pretty and she knew it,' says nurse's aide Linda Bidwell Simcheck, who went to school with the star. 'I'm not saying she was conceited . . . well, she was a little.'

Classmate and sometime boyfriend Lou Severo sees it this way: 'Sharon was the only teenage girl I ever met who was constantly on a diet. She sold hot dogs but she would never eat one. Not that she was ever an ounce overweight. I thought her obsession with watching what she ate was a problem, but the reason behind it was obvious as soon as you talked to her . . . All she cared about was going to Hollywood and being a big movie star. At the time it sounded funny coming from this fifteen-year-old girl who wore too much make-up.

'Even though Sharon boasted she was going to replace Marilyn Monroe, she was an old-fashioned girl who didn't want to date a boy more than once unless he was willing to make a commitment. I worked in a fast food restaurant and I couldn't afford a ring – that ended our relationship. We kept in touch and stayed friends for years. I saw her a few years after she started college and was amazed. She'd completely remade herself as a beauty. A lot of the guys who had dated her casually were sorry they hadn't taken her more seriously.'

Sharon Stone took herself *seriously*. Richard Baker, the former assistant principal at Saegertown High School, said: 'She knew where she wanted to go. She told me and many others she was going to replace Marilyn Monroe.' His wife Pauline, a librarian, recalled: 'Sharon always had the big "A" – for ambition. She saw her way out of Meadville.'

What Stone remembers most about her school days is the

numbing boredom. Even taking part in a MENSA experimental programme for children with high IQs was a drag. She and some other bright students spent half of each school day at nearby Edinboro State College, where they could better exercise their brains. She was also a fledgling actress, taking part in the school's theatre productions.

'She was always confident on-stage and there was a spark, but I never thought, there was no indication, that she was going to be the hottest movie star in the world,' said Richard Baker.

Classmate Randy Schlosser, who now works as a physical therapist, believes all the bad word on Stone was to do with envy: 'I think the girls in the class were simply jealous of Sharon's looks and smarts.'

And Stone was learning all the time about life – and the movies: 'There was only one movie theatre in my hometown, so I saw whatever was there a million times. I loved movies and painting and literature – everything artistic and aesthetic. It all inspired me. But my parents did not put me in a private school, so I didn't have the opportunity to achieve my full potential academically. When I was fifteen I went to high school half a day and college the other half. Then I went to a local college, one that was not very stimulating.

'The dean let me take course overloads and I didn't have to be in all my classes all the time, so long as I maintained a certain grade point average. The classes were very helpful to me, but it soon became clear that I could take a course overload *and* drugs and still be bored. I needed to be in a different environment in order to be inspired to go on with academics. I took a course in the history of modern architecture, in which I learned about Christo. I ended up minoring in modern architecture because it was so inspiring to me to think of artists as architects and architects as artists. It was a revelation that an artist wasn't defined by his medium.

'Of all the arts, I thought I had the least talent as an actor – so I picked it. It was the furthest reach.'

But it wasn't the shortest way out of town.

She was one of only 118 graduating seniors at Saegertown High School in 1975, the year she entered the Miss Crawford County beauty contest. She says someone put her name forward, but most of her classmates and teachers remember Sharon Stone entering Sharon Stone in the pageant . . .

There were no worries in the looks department – Sharon Stone was much more than sweet seventeen. But for some reason – classmates say it was to prove she was displaying her brains as well as her body – for the talent segment she chose to recite the Gettysburg Address.

'It was kinda tough, trying to get her to pull it off with conviction,' said Walter T. Holland, a retired eye surgeon who was her coach. In an attempt to get their contestant to put some emotion into her delivery, Walt Holland's wife Hap took Stone to one side of the stage. 'I explained all about the horrors of the American Civil War to her, in an attempt to get her to put some feeling into the words as she recited them. She seemed to be hanging on my every word. She was animated and nodding, and appeared to be getting the message. We went back over to where my husband was waiting. I smiled and nodded and we were both pleased, for it looked as if Sharon had understood what we were getting at, the seriousness of the subject, the depth of the tragedy of the Civil War.

'Then I started repeating what I'd been saying to her. But then, without a smile on her face, quite solemnly, she interrupted and asked: "Mrs Holland, may I ask you something? Should I wear sparkly stuff in my hair?"'

She did. She became Miss Crawford County. And she went back to Edinboro State College and tried not to be bored.

As Miss Crawford County she was invited to compete for Miss Pennsylvania in Philadelphia. It was an invitation to the outside world, a step out of the Stone Age:

'I'd never been anywhere, done anything. It wasn't until I was a senior in high school that I went on an escalator for the first time. When I went to Philadelphia I still had never been in an elevator.'

She was not placed in the Miss Pennsylvania contest, but one of the judges suggested to her mother, who was acting as her chaperone, that she try modelling. Stone could not contain herself: 'I always wanted to leave – I just had to wait until I could make my escape.'

Dorothy Stone says she was concerned about her daughter at this time, in these teen-woman years. Sharon Stone was frustrated and fed up. Although independent and a loner, she liked a man in her life.

She was seeing Richard Baker Junior, the son of her high school principal, and they shared a love of the school theatre productions and films. Their dates were usually to the show at the town's neon-missing Car-t-n (Carlton) Cinema. Baker was fun, but could be moody. Stone liked a man who wasn't all over her, pestering and bothering her. So she could concentrate on getting on with being famous.

With her mother's help, she went to New York at Christmas 1976–1977, to try for an interview with the Eileen Ford Model Agency. Their Manhattan offices get dozens of girls every day, all wanting to be the new Cindy Crawford or Elle McPherson or Naomi Campbell. Dorothy Stone told her daughter: 'If they don't like you, you can come back here and hit the books.'

Her daughter shot back the reply which emphasises everything about her subsequent super-success: 'If *they* don't like me, I'll just try someplace else.'

She didn't have to. At eighteen, she left Meadville – and Richard Baker Junior – and was on her way to earning $500 a day. For three years she flaunted designer fashions on the world's catwalks, while continuing to study acting.

The Eileen Ford Agency is cautious and careful in looking after their young models and often puts them in 'dormitory' accommodation during training, but Stone almost died trying to be a success. There was constant pressure on her to become thinner. She lived with one of the Ford agents: 'It was very strict. I wasn't allowed to bring sodas into the apartment because soda was bad for me. I was only allowed to have crackers and water. I was a big farmgirl and they were trying to bounce the fat off me. I'm still the fattest thin girl I know. I started modelling, moved out of the agent's apartment, moved downtown in New York and then moved to Europe and continued to model. I lived in Europe, being tortured by Italian playboys, and wondered: "Why am I doing this?" So I packed my bags, moved back to New York and stood in line to try and be in a Woody Allen movie.'

She credits her hometown with helping her survive the pressures of the catwalk game: 'Meadville was a very small town where everyone knew everybody else. I came from a solid, blue-collar family where I learned that good manners take you far. My upbringing left me with a basic way to live . . . That saved my life as a young model in Europe and New York. A lot of the girls I met then became drug addicts and died.'

She was driven and ambitious beyond belief. She went to a 'doctor' in Manhattan who said he had ingredients to take away any bulges: 'They gave me shots every day. They made me feel terribly ill, leaving me weak and dizzy. One day I was so sick I thought I was dying.

'The shots were animal hormones that were meant to change my metabolism. I was shaking all over, I had throbbing headaches. I couldn't walk and my friends had to practically carry me into a doctor's office. He wanted to check me into a hospital. He didn't know what was wrong. I didn't want to tell him I was having hormone shots to make myself skinny. So I just went home and suffered until the effects of the shots wore off. I didn't know what was in them, and then discovered they were made up of sheep embryos and the urine from pregnant women.'

However outlandish and outrageous her efforts to keep her shape may seem, she says they pale against the antics of many of the models she met during her time jetting around from Milan to Paris, New York, London and Tokyo: 'Some of the girls I was with are dead now. The late seventies and early eighties were a very decadent time. People were free-basing cocaine, partying all night long and having wild sex. I wasn't into that. I would go to the clubs all night and drink mineral water. It was like working out for me.' She was getting high on ambition: 'Being a model was a good gig for me. I'm obviously not like your model chick. I don't look like these girls. I can get it up and look good, though I look better on film . . . But I'm not size three, ten-foot-tall perfect. Being in that world always seemed like such a scam to me. I was always uncomfortable. But at the same time I was able to do it and make great money, so that I didn't have to be a starving artist while I studied acting and lost my Pennsylvania accent.'

Her mother was concerned when Stone left home to pursue her modelling career in New York: 'But I was more worried when she went to live in Europe from New York. When I'd go out in the street with her in New York, she'd put her fingers in her mouth and whistle for a cab, and I'd look at her and think: "Who is this girl?" I was frightened to death, but it was like she had been there all her life.'

However, Stone never forgot her roots. While she prospered as a model, doing scores of television commercials, her pining boyfriend Richard Baker Junior married someone else. Brenda Moore already had three daughters and a son by a previous marriage, but that didn't bother Baker Junior. He had become a licensed pilot and a partner in a successful flight training school. The marriage was rocky and friends say he had never really got over his relationship with Stone.

Baker Junior and his wife moved to Carlisle, Ohio, and then at Christmas in 1987 Brenda Baker called the police. Her husband was missing. So was his handgun. He had been very depressed, and she was concerned that he might be going to commit suicide. The patrolmen set off their sirens and gunned their cars to Hook Airport in Carlisle where Baker Junior, thirty-four, kept his planes. They found his station wagon in a hangar. He was in the driver's seat, slumped against the window, having shot himself in the head.

'Sharon was absolutely devastated when she heard of his death,' said Baker's father, adding, 'She and Richard had kept in touch.'

Two years later, Stone went to a high school reunion, where she gave the commencement address. But, before she saw anyone, she met Richard Baker Senior, who said: 'I was deeply moved that she took time out from all that was going on, from the public, to be with me. She was truly a good listener and was trying to help me. We talked for half an hour. When she went back to Hollywood she wrote to me and the letter said: "In whatever state he made his choice, your son made his own choice. And now, perhaps, it is best to respect that choice. For you to allow him to rest in peace means you must try to live in peace and in love with the rest of your beautiful family. And know that my thoughts, my love and my prayers are always with you. Because you, above all my teachers, inspired me to live and to see."'

From the moment she began modelling, Sharon Stone knew it was simply a means to an end. She could make money and continue to attend acting classes and auditions. She says her memories of her three years as a model helped her with her lethal role in *Basic Instinct*. She laughs: 'I would have loved to have killed a lot of art directors and clients I worked with over the years. To have ice-picked them as they came into the changing room every time we were changing . . .'

She became one of the Ford agency's 'Top Ten' models, but detested being an *object*, and regards modelling as a dark period in her life: 'I didn't know the depths of darkness to which I would fall. I made the jump to acting because modelling is so demeaning to the women who do it.'

But the glamorous, international model life was good experience and training for Tinseltown – she learned posture and how to deal with men. She jetted around the world, and the rough edges of small-town Meadville were, like her Pennsylvania accent, smoothed out. 'I still find it hard to believe I have modelled everywhere, from Manhattan to Milan, Paris to Japan, South Africa to Hollywood.' And at twenty, she was desperate for Hollywood, but for movies, not modelling. She had seen style and had lived stylishly in New York and Paris and Milan, but her mind was set on celluloid stardom. It was to be a long but, if generally comfortable, frustrating haul to the top of stardom's shaky ladder.

From her first modelling days she invested in various savings and pension schemes – you can take the girl out of rural Pennsylvania, but not the rainy day ethic out of the girl.

She made it – finally. And would say of her eventual stardom: 'I earned this. I didn't come out here [Hollywood] and say I was the greatest actress in the world right out of the chute. Sometimes I was good, sometimes I was really stinky. They didn't owe me anything. I stayed. I held my place in line. They got to my number – you have to understand that when I got here I was twenty-one and looked sixteen and had this voice and this attitude. There was nowhere for me. The best slot that people felt they could put me in was the bimbo slot. It's because I looked like Barbie.'

Stone was interrupted so it could be pointed out that Barbie Dolls do not have pubic hair. She smiled and put the record straight: 'If you look at any little girl's Barbie she's taken a ballpoint pen and she's drawn pubic hair on it.'

4

Barbie goes to Hollywood

'I *do* know how to travel with only a change of G-strings, a passport, something black and an attitude'
— Sharon Stone, 1992

Sharon Stone, even if only twenty-one, had a feel for the world when she arrived in Hollywood. But not the key to the town. She found it a lonely place, and learned quickly that you have to make your own friends – and luck. She went up for almost every audition she could find. And there were always dozens of other would-be actresses desperate for a role, a line, a walk-on.

She became older and more sophisticated. Even a dozen years later, screenwriter Joe Eszterhas says: 'Sharon is a thousand people and one of them is certainly the little girl from Meadville.'

But she had learned to disguise the little girl beneath a confident charade. And she looked the part: she was stunning, long-legged with cascading blonde hair and, in 1980, something of a teen-tease Farrah Fawcett clone. Woody Allen had finally been accepted as a serious director with his Oscar-winning *Annie Hall* in 1977, in which he starred with his lover Diane Keaton, who gave a quirky display in the title role, a show of stammers and little-girl self-depreciation.

By 1980, he was so revered he sent himself, his critics and fans up in *Stardust Memories*. He played a film director on the

run from all around him, including his women. The film is full
of inside jokes and the harassing mess of his lovelife involving
Charlotte Rampling, Marie-Christine Barrault and Jessica
Harper. Allen's Sandy Bates escapes into his fantasies.

Enter Sharon Stone, who had returned from Milan to New
York to become a movie actress.

Allen needed someone to appear on screen for a fleeting
moment, but still remain in the audiences' mind. 'We had
lots and lots of girls,' he recalled, adding: 'Agents send them
along and hope, of course, that they will get bigger parts in
the picture. Sometimes, they do. But for this scene I needed
someone who would look startling, but not comic-book. I
wanted a *real fantasy* woman,' he laughed, adding: 'We must
have looked at and talked to scores of girls, but Sharon was
the one. I looked at her and thought I would really like her to
kiss me!'

Stone remembers: 'I was one of hundreds sitting in a high
school cafeteria. Woody sat with the casting person and
watched, and when I walked up, the casting person said: "Mr
Allen would like you to stay." I sat there for a while, watching
hundreds of others hand in their pictures. Woody never spoke
to me. After a while I thought: "Fellini should be shooting
this! I'm gonna go now." I did and I got called. They said to
wear white. I was sitting reading a book when Woody came
up to me. He talked for half an hour. We had this weird conversation about infinity because the book I was reading was a
children's book that explained infinity to a child. Woody left
and his assistant came over to me and said: "Hey Woody
really liked you. Would you like to have a part in the movie?"
I'm like, "All Right!! When do I start?"

'I went to wardrobe and they put me in a bombshell dress.
I said: "Wait. Let me explain something – I'm not a bombshell." They didn't see it my way. I played Woody's fantasy.
And that was the beginning of the end.' Stone was Allen's
shimmering wet dream in *Stardust Memories*, which was
filmed in black and white. It gave her tiny scene a *Casablanca*

flavour and, even though it was a blink-and-you'll-miss-it-moment, she was singled out by the critics. Allen as Sandy Bates is taking a train journey when he spots Stone's mystery girl. She has to give him an open mouthed kiss through the window of the train carriage. 'He said he wanted me to kiss the window. He said: "Do it like you were really kissing me." I just really laid it on.'

And turned on the critics and Allen, who said: 'You take a chance on a moment and a person and hope it works. This one did quite wonderfully. All these years later, Sharon's a whole new business but I'd like to work with her again. Maybe we could have a real kiss this time.'

Depends on the deal. 'She'll set goals months and years ahead and everything she does is pointed in that direction,' says horror-schlock director Wes Craven, who introduced the terrifying but incredibly popular Freddy Krueger to the world in *Nightmare on Elm Street* in 1984.

Craven, aka the Sultan of Slash, the Guru of Gore, the Father of Fear, is a specialist in fright films. He directed only the original in the series of *Nightmare on Elm Street* movies, but believes it was his first effort, *The Last House on the Left*, which was the most violent. 'It was a real slap in the face to society,' he said at his rambling home in Santa Monica, California, adding: 'I've never made a film quite so violent or nasty since. We filmed it for $90,000 and it went on to gross more than $20 million.'

He followed up *Last House* with *The Hills Have Eyes*, *Swamp Thing* and then Sharon Stone's *Deadly Blessing*, which is now one of Craven's cult films. He had Stone playing a chemically addicted model who, with a couple of other lookalike model types, was being stalked by a fiendish killer. 'It was strictly *Charlie's Angels* get a scare,' says Stone. But it was also Sharon Stone Gets A Start. It was her first starring role. In June 1990, she was asked about her portrayal of the drug-crazed model and matter of factly replied: 'Not unlike my natural self at the time.'

Craven says he knew she was a winner. 'It's not just hindsight. I've worked with lots and lots of actors at the start of their careers – I *know* the signs. Her signals were all the correct ones. She wasn't looking for an easy way to succeed. She was willing to work, to take classes and do all she could as long as she could be a star.

'Would-be actors and actresses come out to Hollywood all the time and think it is easy, but it's not. You can be the most beautiful girl in the world, but if you can't put presence or charisma or whatever that star "it" is over on screen, it doesn't matter how gorgeous you are.

'Sharon had "it". There was never any question. She's a pit-bull. She'll latch onto something and won't let go. As far as her business is concerned she's the diva queen. And king, I might add.'

The word on Sharon Stone was out in Hollywood. Casting agents dubbed her 'the most beautiful girl in town'. She was being noticed by producers and by others. Sometimes for the wrong reasons.

Beverly Hills Madam Alex Adams had her eyes on her as a potential 'girl' who would make $10,000 a night sleeping with some of her international clients. Stone herself was quickly the victim of the casting couch and is quite hilarious about her first encounter with it.

'The first time I turned down a studio executive who wanted to sleep with me, he screamed: "You'll never work in this town again!!" I thought it was the funniest thing I'd ever *heard*. When a well-known producer opened his zipper and went to pull out his thing during a meeting I thought that was the funniest thing I'd ever *seen*. I mean, hey, if you're going to act out a movie, couldn't you at least act out a better one? I'm a trophy to a lot of men.'

Of course, she was even more so in the 1990s, following *Basic Instinct*.

But in the early 1980s she was the new girl in a town run by and running with blasé and cynical men. Studio bosses, famous actors, directors and producers *expect* women chasing success to grant their every sexual whim. Stone wasn't above playing the game – but on her terms.

And because of that, there was much gossip about her. She found herself a small apartment on Camden Avenue in Beverly Hills and set about worrying about work, not men. She was involved with the Tracy Roberts Acting Workshop, the Harvey Lembeck Improvisational Comedy Workshop and studied privately with actor Allan Rich. And all the time there were voice and dance classes. Each day was regimented. Sharon Stone had decided there was no such thing as a free lunch. She'd been brought up to understand that work equalled gain.

'In New York I had studied Method acting [with Marilyn Freid and Jack Waltzer] but I don't think I really learned anything until I began studying with Roy London in Los Angeles. He has an intellectual approach to acting. He doesn't tell you to lie down on the floor and pretend to be a piece of bacon frying.'

She also learned other lessons: 'In Hollywood you can be tall, you can be blonde, you can be pretty, but you can't be smart. You can't have too many opinions. Being blonde is a great excuse when you are having a bad day: "I'm blonde, I can't help it – I'm just feeling very blonde today." I've been called a Vargas girl.' She laughs to herself about the Vargas drawings of pneumatically stacked women in American men's magazines and adds: 'I do try to lie on my back wearing very sheer black lingerie as often as possible.'

More mundane outfits were required for *Bay City Blues*, but so were her 'beautiful blonde' looks. To Sharon Stone, it seemed the perfect opportunity, a stepping-stone to stardom. The television series was the brainchild of Steve Bochco and his associates, the creators of the long-running *Hill Street Blues*. It was scheduled on prime-time on America's giant NBC network and she had the central role of a baseball player's wife. But, like so many other TV shows, it didn't work. She had a contract for twenty-one episodes, so was secure financially but, instead of the priceless exposure of being beamed every week into America's homes, she was looking for work.

She found it. Some good. Some not so good. She won a small part in French director–writer–producer Claude Lelouch's *Bolero* (known in France as *Les Unes et Les Autres*) and worked with James Caan, Geraldine Chaplin, Jean-Claude Brialy and Robert Hossein. It was self-indulgent Lelouch and some versions of the film ran to more than six hours. It was not a star vehicle for Sharon Stone.

The very American *Irreconcilable Differences* in 1984 offered far more opportunity – and she accepted it. The credits read: 'Starring Ryan O'Neal, Shelley Long, Drew Barrymore in *Irreconcilable Differences*'; below the title it went on: 'also starring: Sam Wanamaker, Allen Garfield and Introducing Sharon Stone'.

It was impressive, but intense company to be in. Shelley Long had left her secure and award-winning role as barmaid Diane in *Cheers* and needed to prove herself on the big screen. O'Neal, as well as being desperate for a hit movie, was also awaiting the arrival of his son Redmond by former 'Charlie's Angel' Farrah Fawcett, with whom he had lived since 1979.

And the film they were making was Tinseltown-touchy in subject matter. 'Everybody in Hollywood was scared to make a movie about a Hollywood director who leaves his wife and kid for a starlet. Everybody was going to think it was about them,' says O'Neal.

'Was it based on anyone in particular? Oh, yes. Though when I outlined the story to Gregory Peck, he said: "I know any number of directors who have done that."'

Irreconcilable Differences was written by husband and wife team Charles Shyer and Nancy Meyers, who also were responsible for Goldie Hawn's hugely successful *Private Benjamin* in 1980. It tells the tale of film professor Albert Brodsky (O'Neal), who goes from academia to the Academy

Awards after one hit film and ends up abandoning his wife (Long) and daughter (Barrymore) to concentrate on making Sharon Stone's waitress Blake Chandler a star. Barrymore (in a performance nagging the memory of eight-year-old Tatum O'Neal playing opposite her father in her Oscar-winning role in 1973's *Paper Moon*), as the ten-year-old daughter, sues her parents for divorce.

Despite the cute premise, it was Stone as the girl who sleeps her way to the top who stole the movie. The besotted Brodsky agrees to Blake Chandler's demands to star her in a musical remake of *Gone With The Wind*. She tells him: 'I've already written half my songs.' She then purrs: 'I've always wanted to play Scarlett O'Hara since Junior High.' They make a mega-flop entitled 'Atlanta'.

Charles Shyer screened several movies for Stone, whose role he felt was pivotal to the film, including classics like Cary Grant and Rosalind Russell in *His Girl Friday* and Bogart and Lauren Bacall in *To Have and Have Not*, a movie she would recall for a later role. The director said: 'I wanted Sharon to see Bacall's debut. I thought she was someone who was going to reach the same heights in the movies. She had a gift for timing and comic delivery. She had all the right qualities – and the determination to make a success of her role and the movie. She wanted all of us to be winners.'

Stone herself is more wicked in her recollections. In a tilt at some awful musical comedies made by Cybill 'Moonlighting' Shepherd, she says: 'I played an actress who doesn't realise that every time she breaks into song in a musical she's really stupid. The studio screened two Cybill Shepherd movies for me.'

Whatever the reason, they did the trick. Stone received some of her best reviews – of all the 1980s. Scot Haller in America's *People* magazine wrote: 'When Stone belts a brassy Streisand-like number amid the corpses after the burning of Atlanta the comedy shows a fresh sensibility.' Others talked of a 'breakthrough performance' and 'stunning debut' and

'Sharon Stone steals the movie from Shelley Long and O'Neal'.

For Sharon Stone they were wonderful days. 'The film was too fun. I loved doing it. But even although I got a tremendous amount of attention and great reviews from the part, my career was really improperly managed at the time. The mistakes that were made cost me many years of having to make shitty movies.'

For Ryan O'Neal, who had moved on from the mother of all television soaps, *Peyton Place,* to an Oscar nomination and matinee idol fame with *Love Story* in 1970, the film won him his best reviews in years – nine years since the expensive box-office disaster of director Stanley Kubrick's *Barry Lyndon.*

'I loved the movie, so I did it for no salary just points [a percentage of profits]. It was made for under $6 million, so they didn't have the money to pay our usual rates. Still, I think it is some of my best work – maybe I should work like that more often. We all had something going on the film. We were trying to prove what we could do. Sharon was exceptional in a tough role, and there was no doubt that one day she was going to be a remarkable star.

'Did I have any advice for her? Everybody gives you different advice. When I made *The Wild Rovers* with Bill Holden, I asked him: "What acting advice can you give me, Bill?" After all, he'd made more than seventy movies and I was just beginning. You know what he said? "Have a good tan." He told me that was the advice Cary Grant had given him when he asked the same question.'

Sharon Stone wouldn't agree with that. She believes that her work, rather than her looks, won in the end: 'I'm one of the few blondes in the business who has trained hard dramatically and comedically. You have to work hard, because when you walk into an auditorium you had better have something to give the casting director. Auditions are nerve-racking enough. One of my strong points was that I'm so chameleon-like in my looks that it's hard for producers to pinpoint my age. I'm also relatively articulate. You could say I'm a little smarter than the average bear.'

Cuter too.

She moved on. Professionally. And personally. But it wasn't easy on either front.

5

Marriage,
Rock and AIDS

'I wanted to be the perfect wife'
– Sharon Stone, 1992

Rock Hudson was dying from AIDS when Sharon Stone met him for the first time. They were co-starring in 1984 in a high-profile television movie entitled *The Vegas Strip Wars*, during which she was to get her first close-up view of star power and its benefits and terrors. *The Vegas Strip Wars* was a vehicle for Hudson, who had moved smoothly from international film stardom to the same status on television; his *Macmillan and Wife* series with Susan St James was one of the most popular and profitable series ever made by Universal-MCA.

But now this beefcake actor, who had wooed and won some of the world's most beautiful women on screen, was dying from 'the gay plague'. Hudson's death from AIDS on 2 October 1985 did more worldwide to bring public attention to the disease than anything that had gone before. President Reagan, who had never publicly mentioned the word 'AIDS' at that time, had telephoned his friend and colleague in hospital to wish him well. Hudson's close friend Elizabeth Taylor, who had co-starred with him in *Giant*, for which he had won an Oscar nomination, was moved by his death to begin her tireless efforts for AIDS research funding.

By 1984, Hudson was acutely aware that his life was ebbing away. But he was an actor. A star. And he would continue to perform. He contracted to appear on *Dynasty* – which he would later call 'Die Nasty' – as the love interest of Linda Evans' Krystle Carrington.

Sharon Stone saw similarities in the prime-time soap and *The Vegas Strip Wars*. 'There were lots of things alike between us – money, crime and passion. My character Sara was a cigarette girl who seduces Rock. He played Neil Caine, who was the patriarch of the casino operation. I'd say she was like Lauren Bacall in *To Have and Have Not*, in that she used all her tools to seduce him.

'Being a cigarette girl is just one stop in her life. She's way on top of her situation. She's totally in control. And by seducing Rock, the most powerful figure in town, it's a victory for her manipulation.'

And, in real life, a ludicrous scenario. Throughout his career, Hudson was concerned about the rumours and talk that he was gay. It was not his image. But with his life running away from him 1984, he found solace wherever he could. And Sharon Stone wanted to help. Which meant listening to Hudson's story. It was an education for her. For, if she was the sex-babe bombshell of the 1980s, all those years earlier, Hudson had been the male equivalent. They didn't want him to act the part – just look it. And he did.

Roy Scherer Junior was born on 17 November 1925, in Winnekta, Illinois. His father left him and his mother Kay when he was seven years old and she later married a labourer called Wally Fitzgerald. Hudson told Stone how he was, like her, something of an outcast during his schooldays. He was tall, 6ft 4ins, skinny and uncoordinated and took beatings from his stepfather. After his mother divorced Fitzgerald, Hudson shared her bed in an apartment over a shop while she worked as a housekeeper. He spent two years during World War II in the Navy, and then landed in Hollywood where he met radio producer Ken Hodge. It was Hodge who, along with some friends, thought up the macho name Rock Hudson for the boy from Illinois; Ken who introduced him to the infamously gay

Hollywood agent Henry Willson. In 1948, Hudson appeared in *Fighter Squadron*, and then went on a seven-year contract with Universal Studios. Away from the movies, he met actor George Nader and Mark Miller, a gay couple who would be his friends and influence him for most of his life.

As Sharon Stone today has to deal with her 'sex goddess' label, the young Hudson had to cope with being created as a romantic leading man. The Universal Studios publicity machine had him pose in topless photographs with captions like: 'What a MAN!' Then, after *Magnificent Obsession* in 1954 – thirty years before he co-starred with Sharon Stone – he was caged. The weepie movie in which he played a surgeon who blinded a woman, Ronald Reagan's first wife Jane Wyman, was silly but successful. His fan mail became enormous.

As did the interest in his sex life. Happily for him and the studio for whom he was making millions, he became involved with his agent's secretary Phyliss Gates. He needed a wife. She liked the glamorous life. It was an appropriate arrangement but ended in divorce. She maintained they had a full sexual relationship and has always denied all rumours of lesbianism. But it was certainly a marriage of convenience for Hudson, who went on to greater fame starring with Doris Day in movies like *Pillow Talk*, *Lover Come Back* and *Send Me No Flowers*.

But what fascinated Sharon Stone most was how Hudson's seemingly glowing career could suddenly stop. From superstardom, he was suddenly a resident of Jurassic Park. Disillusioned, he took roles in action films like *Ice Station Zebra* in 1968 and *The Undefeated* with John Wayne, a year later. He also indulged in all sorts of other action at The Castle, the home Universal Studios had bought him on Beverly Crest Drive in Beverly Hills. The Spanish-style mansion was filled with sculptures of young boys, and described by one Hudson associate as 'early butch'. When questioned about his gay side being obvious, Hudson told confidantes: 'There's a little girl in me that I just trample to death.'

What he wanted was a stable homosexual relationship. He attempted it with twenty-five-year-old Lee Carrington, a hunky blond extra on the Western television series *The Virginian*. But the lad was disappointed in Hudson: 'He was so big and towered over me. I wanted him to be a father figure but he wasn't. He was shy – when the phone rang, he'd grab a cigarette. He drank too much and was easily controlled by his hangers-on.'

Another blond, twenty-three-year-old Jack Coates, moved into The Castle in 1967 and stayed for four years. In 1971, Hudson was upset to learn of gossip and even media mentions that he had 'married' TV situation comedy star Jim Nabors. Then Tom Clark, a former MGM Studios Press agent who was the same age as Hudson, moved in with him in 1973. They were to be friends until the end. Clark and Hudson spent many, many boozy nights together with their toast: 'Fuck him – I hope he dies.'

In the seventies Hudson had successful theatre tours with the musical *I Do! I Do* and *Camelot*. In 1979, he met gay author Armistead Maupin, who created *Tales of the City* as a daily serial in the *San Francisco Chronicle*, then turned it into a series of books and, in 1993, a serial for BBC television. Maupin took Hudson on a tour of the rougher gay bars in San Francisco and recalled: 'It was ironic. I'm standing with the man who was *the* sex symbol of the world for two decades, and nobody's paying any attention to him. We could walk through the place like two women – invisible.'

Then, the tragedy and the sadness. Hudson found a new lover in Marc Christian, blond, blue-eyed and Hudson's fantasy of perfection. Hudson's friend George Nader said: 'It was like a caricature of the aging star. After thirty-five years, this is what's left: a man whose cheeks are starting to fall in, who doesn't look good, sitting with a guy half his age that he doesn't like and who's using him.'

At the same time, he was making *The Vegas Strip Wars* and *Dynasty* . . . and losing weight and suffering night sweats.

When he attended the Oscars in 1984, his dinner-jacket had to be taken in with safety pins.

His friends, the Reagans, posed with Hudson in a photograph where a sore is clear on his neck. At times, he had so many lesions on his body he could not walk around in clothes; it was too painful. Later, doctors told him he had Kaposi's sarcoma, a skin disease linked to AIDS. He went to Paris for treatment and at the same time signed on for *Dynasty*. He appeared in nine episodes of the series which starred John Forsythe, Joan Collins and Linda Evans, who would later be terrified that their screen kisses might have infected her.

It was on 15 July in Carmel, California, where Clint Eastwood presided as Mayor for two years, that it became clear that Hudson was dying. He had been seen on *Dynasty* and appeared quite chunky in *The Vegas Strip Wars*, but that day he looked as good as dead. He had turned up as a guest on his old friend Doris Day's new syndicated cable television show. That day, you could see the enormous effort it was taking him just to speak. 'I only came for Doris,' he said, through a weak smile.

Sharon Stone says that her favourite story about Hudson, the man who had hidden his sexuality for years, involved his housekeeper who told him: 'Talk about coming out of the closet – you came out of the *house*.'

But it's a painful subject for Stone because she became so friendly with Hudson that he agreed to be the godfather of her children – when she had them. For during the filming of their TV movie she also met her soon-to-be husband, the programme's producer Michael Greenburgh.

The trio became close friends. Stone and Greenburgh were truly, madly and crazily in love. 'I loved my husband from the minute I laid eyes on him,' says Stone. Hudson became the father-figure to them that he had never been able to be in his own personal life. Stone and Greenburgh's madcap affair entertained him, kept his mind off other matters.

'Rock was an extraordinarily brave and generous man. We became very good friends. It was a special time for me,' said Stone, who also became friends with James Earl Jones during the production. 'You know, he also agreed to be godfather to the children we never had.'

Their marriage didn't last much longer than the rest of Rock Hudson's life.

But back then, Sharon Stone was blindly in love. She spent filming breaks on the phone to her family, telling them she had 'met the man of my dreams' and that, yes, they could expect a wedding in the very near future. She told her father to buy a new suit and her mother 'to get something very special to wear' for her wedding day. When talking about all the wedding arrangements she regressed to the little girl from Meadville. Her parents say her voice echoed excitement in every conversation they had.

On 18 August 1984, she and Greenburgh, who was then thirty-three, married in Erie, Pennsylvania, in a small, town ceremony and then moved into a rented apartment in Beverly Hills. They had the trinkets of budding Tinseltown success. She whizzed about town in her BMW 325E, while he gunned his Alfa Romeo to appointments. They collected art, furs, crystal, and were a way-above-average-in-earning-power couple. Greenburgh (who would later work for Henry 'The Fonz' Winkler's production company on the 'MacGYVER' action-adventure television series) is a careful man. He opened cash reserve accounts for them both (account number: L625–19–41) and also invested in M and K Mainstreet Partners and in a company called Washington Partners. They were all steady investments.

'My husband was a real straight guy and we had a sort of squeaky-clean little relationship. I wanted us to be the perfect couple. He had been the captain of the football team and the golf team. I wanted to be the perfect wife.

'Like everyone else, I wanted to be normal, I wanted life to be easier. But I was very rigid – I wanted to be perfect. Maybe

I thought being perfect, being better, was being different from whom I actually was. It took me a long time to understand that being who I am is enough.'

Some friends who remember going to the Stone–Greenburgh apartment say it was a home where everything was in its place. 'It was like one of those apartments they show you to see what yours *could* be like if you rent or buy from them,' said Tina Livingstone, who worked as a production associate with Greenburgh, but she added: 'That wasn't their life. They were both really into movies and movie-making. They'd see every film almost on the day it was released. They had two things going for themselves – each other and the movies. That's all they seemed to care about.'

Then they went to Africa.

6

Jungle Fever

'I had an agent that sold me out'
– Sharon Stone, 1994

Zimbabwe is a country of natural beauty and an inspired choice for the location filming of a remake of H. Rider Haggard's *King Solomon's Mines*. The film was produced by Menahem Golan and Yoram Globus through their Cannon Group Incorporated, which in the 1980s produced a string of successful but ridiculous action-adventure style movies. It was appropriate that they should be involved in this legendary tale about 'wealth beyond the imagination of men', supposedly buried in the heart of the African jungle. For this attempt to cash in on the success of Steven Spielberg/Harrison Ford's *Indiana Jones* films – and its subsequent sequel *Allan Quartermain and the Lost City of Gold* – was all about money. This was a scavenging safari, endorsed only by some veteran talent.

For Sharon Stone it was *Carry On Up The Jungle*. The Cannon Group saw the wisdom of getting two films out of their investment in the overseas location, and Michael Greenburgh was a producer on the *Allan Quartermain* segment. But as footage for both films was mingled he was, at first, happily stuck in Africa with his relatively new wife . . . who quickly realised she was not a happy camper.

'I had an agent that sold me out,' she insists, although the

Creative Artists Agency of Beverly Hills who represented her at that time will not comment on her statement. Stone goes on: 'They had a deal with their producer. I thought the movie was horrible and they said: "We'll waive our commission because this is good for you." They told me it was important to be *starring* a movie . . . I spent a year in Africa, and that'll put your career to a grinding halt.'

It didn't do much for Richard Chamberlain, either. Like Rock Hudson, he had been a romantic leading man for many, many years when Stone worked with him. Chamberlain became a household name overnight when he was cast as 'Dr Kildare' in 1961. There were 132 episodes running an hour and 58 half-hour shows. After the long run of the medical drama and several Hollywood films, he says he 'escaped' to London where he won critical raves for a series of stage productions. He buried the *Dr Kildare* tag permanently with his 1969 performance as Hamlet – until then, the only other American actor to play the Prince of Denmark on a British stage was John Barrymore.

He then returned to American television in high-rated and respected mini-series like *Shogun*, *The Thorn Birds* and *The Bourne Identity*, making him a Robert Redford of the living-room. A classic leading man, he was the image of the White Hunter Allan Quartermain.

It was a pity about the script. The producers had tried to hedge their bets by rounding up many of the usual suspects for such a project, and the cast included trademark nasty Herbert Lom as an arrogant German and the bulky Welsh actor – and *Indiana Jones* regular – John Rhys-Davies, taking the money for playing a scurrilous Turk. The director was J. Lee-Thompson, who had been responsible for many major movies, including the classic *The Guns of Navarone* in 1961. Thompson, a British director, had worked with Yul Brynner, Tony Curtis, Charlton Heston, Gregory Peck, Anthony Quinn, David Niven, Charles Bronson and Robert Mitchum, and Sharon Stone – the blonde with the brain – was going to learn everything she could.

'It wasn't easy for any of us, but Sharon really wanted to gain from our experience in the jungle,' said Thompson, adding: 'She was plucky.' 'But not lucky,' she later responded to that remark. They started filming on 6 January 1985, in Harare, Zimbabwe. Sharon Stone as Jesse Huston has hired Chamberlain's Quartermain to find her missing archaeologist father Professor Huston and, of course, they find themselves tangling with brigands, kidnappers, salivating cannibals and crocodiles, steaming lava pits and all the other ingredients audiences expect from such thrill-and-spill jungle tales. Britain's swashbuckling actor Stewart Granger, who died in 1993, starred in the 1950 *King Solomon's Mines* (Cedric Hardwicke was the original hero in 1937) and took a special interest in the film. He told me: 'That Chamberlain fellow doesn't even wear his hat correctly. I liked the girl though – I wouldn't mind being in the jungle with her.' Granger, who swore he made love to his *King Solomon's Mines* co-star Deborah Kerr in a tree, was in his mid-seventies and boasted: 'They should have put me in the picture. I could have dealt with her.'

Possibly not. Sharon Stone was, as they say in America, pissed. That is, intoxicated by rage, not alcohol. She's tossed off remarks that she was 'simply a bad hairdo running through the jungle' to describe her feelings about the films, but she was truly miserable. There seemed no way out of, what was increasingly apparent to her, a mess. Cannon wanted two movies out of one – and blood out of Stone.

She had to deal with a python weighing 80lbs that reared its head when she approached: 'I have no affinity for snakes, so I ran backwards from it – and into two leopards. I have always had a rapport for cats. I feel akin to them. The leopards were a better option for me than that big snake. They seemed to feel the same way, for they tried to lick my face.'

The elements and the natives weren't so friendly. Zimbabwe was in the throes of political unrest during the filming of *King Solomon's Mines* and paralysed by the worst

storms in the country's history. Torrential rain turned tropical
streams into swollen, muddy torrents, making filming for
Stone, her co-stars and crew a life-threatening experience.
Every day. The film set was only four hours' drive from
Bulawayo, where the graves of six tourists (two of them
Americans who had been kidnapped in 1982) were discovered. Prime Minister Robert Mugabe had ordered the Army to
cordon off the city. And in Harare, where Stone was staying,
there was increasing tension about the elections set for May
1985. In the former Rhodesia, political and tribal factions were
violently mixing their views. They had abducted community
leaders and teachers, burned a couple who lived on a farm, set
fire to shops and pulled passengers from passing trains and
killed them.

'The conditions were very difficult,' said production executive Liz Odendal, adding: 'We had the constant interruptions
of twice-daily rains and the thunderstorms that struck so
often accounted for long, long days. Richard and Sharon and
the rest of the cast and crew were working from 5 a.m. to
7.30 p.m. most days.'

'We'd spend hours at a time, watching the rain and jump-
ing with each thunderbolt,' recalls Stone. 'We all became tense
and twitchy.'

One of the main sets for the film was the village of
Tongola – a $1-million replica of a Sudanese town. The three-
year drought which had been hurting Zimbabwe, and was
forecast to go on for at least another year had broken and
Tongola had become a swamp. The merchant square was a
quagmire. Every day a scene had to be moved indoors. Sacks
of sand were needed to soak up the water, so that the camera
'dollies' could stand upright. Palm trees, not indigenous to the
area and brought in for filming, took root and flourished in
the swampy ground. Even the cobs of sweetcorn on the walls
of the set started sprouting.

Stone and the crew made fun for themselves – anything to
pass the time – as the rain belted down. They held 'regattas',

using small boats built from pieces of bark and twine, launching them on the flooded set and betting on which one would stay afloat longest.

And the voodoo talk began. The native extras maintained that the film set had been built on an ancient burial ground, and the film-makers had not asked the Spirit's permission to put it there. The torrential rain was their Spirit's curse. J. Lee-Thompson brought calm to the set by asking Chamberlain and Stone and the rest of the cast and crew quietly to acknowledge the Spirit's presence.

The political situation was not as easy to contain. The Zimbabwe Government provided incredible security during the production – they were keen for more location filming to boost their flagging economy – but it meant that Stone and the rest of the production company could not travel around much, and only managed one trip to the Victoria Falls.

With the weather and the tension, many people fell sick and there was the constant threat of malaria. Nearly one hundred people had been killed in the storms. Stone took antimalarial tablets and only drank water sealed in plastic bottles supplied by the Government. What Stone – and Chamberlain – didn't realise at first was that their enterprise was more polluted than the water.

For Chamberlain, the outing as a swashbuckling white hunter seemed a nice antidote to his conscience-ravaged priest in *The Thorn Birds*. He recalled: 'It seemed wonderful not to be so deadly serious all the time. It seemed a perfectly good movie to be making and Sharon Stone was completely professional and delightful. We got on rather well, despite the conditions.'

They met – on screen – in a cannibals' cooking-pot. 'We were both about to be boiled for dinner,' says Chamberlain, adding: 'And the story took off from there. It was a fun script – in the genre of Indiana Jones and the *Raiders of the Lost Ark*.' He said that hopefully. And vainly. This was bargain-basement adventure. And it all became too much for Sharon Stone.

'My husband was a producer of the movie. At the time, I was a very uptight girl, a real goody-goody. My marriage was falling apart and the pressure of that was just enormous for me . . . I'm sure I was a bitch. But if you see that I spent a year of my life in Africa and *King Solomon's Mines* and *Allan Quartermain* are what I've got to show for it, I have a right to be pissed . . . So maybe the people on the films didn't like me sometimes. Tough shit. Michael was producing one of the movies, and that always sets up an uncomfortable situation for everybody. Making those films was incredibly destructive to my marriage because we were both locked in the nightmare of making horrible movies for people who didn't give a shit what we were doing anyway . . . I was panic-stricken because I was months in Africa making movies I knew were destroying my career. I was constantly trying to push and provoke everybody to make it a good movie. My marriage was falling apart. The movie was going to be bad. I'm sure I was a bitch.'

As the weeks stretched into months, the other players in these particular films certainly felt that. They wanted relief. They found it during the filming of the cooking-pot scene where Stone's heroine is about to be boiled alive by cannibals. There were 1,621 extras and 67 dancers swirling around the cooking-pot scene. They had not been served their normal lunch of nyama (meat) and satza (porridge) and vegetables, but were paid a fee to buy their own meal later, so they would look hungry. Stone was to be seen in the equivalent of a hot tub. Her bad mouth and bitchy attitude had preceded her to the water. One of the crew had peed in her bath-water.

She explains the yellowish bath water by repeating the difficult circumstances. And she goes on: 'I could *do* nice, but it's just not as much fun. Being nice isn't my biggest goal in life. I'm trying to be honest about who I am and that's not always nice. I'm not always the world's cheerleader. On a movie, when an actress bitches about wardrobe, food, the director, the hours, the *anything*, it's because we are insecure about our work. The more trained I get, the more secure I get in my work, the easier I am to get along with on set.'

She got out of Africa as soon as possible, and slipped into 'stupid B-movie after B-movie where the women weren't based on any that we have ever known. They were on drugs, on alcohol or insane. My smalltown, blue-collar upbringing put the brakes on my ambition. After a certain point I became complacent. I had a job. I worked regularly. I did three pictures a year. I travelled, I bought a house. It wasn't my dream, OK. But then I went: "I hate my life, I hate my life".' So, she changed it.

She was still stuck in Africa when Rock Hudson died and that only compounded her depression.

Her marriage was a joke: 'I came from a small town and grew up with an idealistic view of men and relationships. I was quite shy, believe it or not. I looked up to men as being the breadwinners and the decision-makers and I thought of marriage as my future. I have realised I am not the marrying kind. Once it goes all wrong, you think: "Hey, maybe I need to re-examine all this." I was not getting anywhere in my career and my private life was a complete and utter mess. When I moved to Los Angeles I accepted it was going to be tough – I just had to hang in there, making my mistakes along with everyone else. Marriage was one of them. I now accept that I don't have a private life. I'm not a kid on dates and demand too little from a man to be really interesting. I have my own life, career, independence and money so the things that women typically seem to need from a man I do not need.'

Sharon Stone made these remarks in 1993, but seven years earlier they would not have been the same. Michael Greenburgh was not the Husband From Hell, but he was not the man she wanted to spend the rest of her life with. On 26 October 1986, he drove his Alfa Romeo away from their apartment for the last time. They had been together for twenty-six months – many of them in Africa.

Greenburgh moved into apartment 405 North on 515
Ocean Avenue in Santa Monica, taking with him his memories of Sharon Stone, a share of their investments, his
collection of silver and personal items like some artwork by
Californian artist John Anderson.

Their separation was made official in the white-painted
Main Street Santa Monica Superior Court on 20 January 1987,
when Judge Jill Robbins approved the dissolution of their
marriage. It was amicable. It was legal. And for both of them,
reflecting back on their marriage, it was the right thing to do.

Sharon Stone decided to do something about her professional and private life. Men she found she could control, but
work was a different matter: 'The advice I was always given
was to keep making films and finally one would click.' She
went up for the Glenn Close role in *Fatal Attraction* and didn't
even get as far as auditioning or reading with Michael
Douglas. Kim Basinger got to play photo-journalist Vicki Vale
opposite Michael Keaton's Batman. And Madonna, who
would later feel threatened by Sharon Stone's film success,
nabbed the role of the super-sexy chanteuse Breathless
Mahoney – and Warren Beatty – in *Dick Tracy*; Sharon Stone
would later also toy with Warren Beatty.

But for the moment it was *Police Academy 4*. Not
Shakespeare, but also not financially silly. The first three *Police
Academy* films had grossed half a billion dollars by 1987. The
films were not only popular in America. Of the movies which
made him a multi-millionaire, producer Paul Maslansky says:
'The overseas grosses have been so good it's almost worth
making them for the foreign market alone.'

Police Academy 4 was derided by the critics, but immediately became America's top earning film. Video sales and
rentals for the *Police Academy* movies are on most Top Ten
lists. Sharon Stone may not have received ecstatic reviews but
she got exposure.

'We kept the pictures constantly good-natured, not venal,
not mean-spirited,' says Maslansky, adding, 'And in each one

we've delivered four or five jokes people talk about – jokes like the cop who is asked to help get a cat out of a tree, and responds by pulling out his Magnum .44 and shooting it down.'

David Graf, who worked on *Irreconcilable Differences* with Stone, plays gun-happy Officer Tackleberry in the series and has another theory: 'We had the prerequisite tits and ass. The films make fun of authority but not of being a policeman. Cops didn't hate the films.' For Sharon Stone, it was a chance to move on. In *Police Academy 4: Citizens on Patrol*, she played 'gorgeous journalist' Clare Matson, who gets to exchange wisecracks with star Steve Guttenberg's policeman Carey Mahoney.

'When I took *Police Academy* I really needed a break from my life. I also really needed a job! It changed me tremendously – for the good, really for the good. I worked with twelve stand-up comedians every day. Not actors, but stand-up comedians. You've no idea what a joy it is to go into a room and hang out with these people – the brilliance and the politically astute, fun, intellectual, strange, inspirational conversations you'll have with them. After Africa it was a wonderful antidote.'

As was *War and Remembrance*, the longest (30 hours) most expensive ($110 million) television mini-series ever made. Stone rated a major credit in the series which starred Robert Mitchum, Jane Seymour, John Gielgud, Victoria Tennant, Hart Bochner, Peter Graves and cameo appearances by Robert Hardy as Churchill, E. G. Marshall as Eisenhower, Ralph Bellamy as Roosevelt and Steven Berkoff as Hitler.

The series took longer to film than World War II itself, and involved 2,070 scenes shot on 757 locations across the world, employing more than 44,000 actors and extras. *War and Remembrance* picked up where *The Winds of War* left off. Mitchum's Victor 'Pug' Henry takes command of a cruiser after the Japanese attack on Pearl Harbor. He also pursues his platonic affair with Victoria Tennant's British beauty while his wife Rhoda (Polly Bergen) engages in a string of love affairs. Pug's Jewish daughter-in-law Natalie Jastrow (Jane Seymour) and her Uncle Aaron (John Gielgud) are caught up in the Holocaust. Producer-director Dan Curtis went further than any film-maker had, at that time, in showing the atrocities of the death camps. Steven Spielberg, with his black and white images in *Schindler's List*, in 1994, made the horrors even more vivid.

Against all the history of the War, Curtis attempted to reflect the human stories: Sharon Stone played Pug Henry's daughter-in-law Janice, the well-bred and educated daughter of a prominent United States Senator. Although madly in love with husband Warren (Michael Woods), the War sends her into an affair with the libidinous Naval Lieutenant 'Lady' Aster played by Barry Bostwick.

'We were all so happy to be part of the series,' says Bostwick. 'Everyone had a tremendous commitment to the show. Sharon, like all of us, really felt she was involved in something important. Our scenes were cogs in the whole enterprise. I think Sharon felt her career was moving in the right direction.'

'It was a marvellous experience for me,' says Stone, adding, 'One that I was proud to be part of. I think that was when I started, possibly subconsciously, reassessing my values. But I wanted to work, so I took the movies that were available to me. I took classes and I just kept working at my craft.'

By 1986, Chuck Binder had taken over as her manager. Together they went after the big roles.

7

Beautiful Blonde

'I played a beautiful blonde married to Steven Seagal
about which I have no comment'
– Sharon Stone on her 1988 movie, *Above the Law*

With Sharon Stone as the sex symbol of the nineties, the
action-man crown belonged to Steven Seagal. He was the
martial arts expert appointed to take over the starring roles in
shoot 'em up adventure films from the aging Clint Eastwood,
Charles Bronson and karate-kicking Chuck Norris, while also
providing box-office competition for Sylvester Stallone and
Arnold Schwarzenegger.

He was to teach Sharon Stone a lot. And not karate or his
own speciality, the Japanese art of aikido. It was more about
manipulation and control.

Seagal – like Stone would do later – suddenly emerged as a
superstar. And was greeted as a man of mystery – something
which he exploited to its full potential. When Hollywood
started calling him a star of the future, he played the part.
Sharon Stone believes he did it too well.

Her friends say that her experience making *Above the Law* –
entitled *Nico* for its British cinema release – which was
Seagal's film debut, devastated her. She has not been persuaded to talk about it since *Basic Instinct*, but before her star
vehicle was released, she did comment: 'I've worked with
nightmarish people. I've been on a movie with an actor who
was so unbelievably vicious it was astonishing to watch. I

learned that in this business there is a "Plan A", in which you become successful by living and acting with a lot of integrity. Then there's "Plan B", where you sell your soul to the Devil and become successful. In Hollywood "Plan A" and "Plan B" patrons mingle. Because I find it hard to distinguish one from the other I sometimes got really burned.'

Seagal demonstrated to her how perseverance and determination can pay off and pay out. He is 6ft 4ins tall, lean, with a tough but handsome profile and well-connected. Californian-born Seagal (pronounced See-GAL) was living in Japan in the late 1970s, where he taught aikido, and claims to have been recruited by the CIA. In 1987, he returned to America and started Aikido Ten Shin Dojo, a martial arts centre in West Hollywood, where he taught students including celebrities like Sean Connery, James Coburn and the late James Mason. He used the name Shigemichi Take – Japanese for 'the road to prosperity' – for his classes. He got to know the right people, including Michael Ovitz, the head of the Creative Artists Agency and credited with being the most powerful man in Hollywood, and Terry Semel, President of Warner Brothers Studios. He also signed up with Paul Bloch, who runs the Entertainment Division of the high-profile public relations company Rogers and Cowan. And to get the 'package' really marketable, he also managed to divorce his Japanese wife Miyako Fujitani, by whom he had two children, and marry British actress and model Kelly Le Brock who was 'The Woman In Red'. His first wife, who was forty-seven in 1994, now teaches martial arts in Osaka, Japan, and has custody of their son Kentaro, who was nineteen in 1994, and daughter Ayako, who was fifteen.

Seagal had equipped himself with all the correct accessories for stardom. He says of Ovitz, whom he taught martial arts: 'Michael was very interested in putting me out there. He believed in me. He thought that I had something very special.' Modestly, he says he got a similar reaction from Terry Semel at Warners: 'He liked my look, he liked my charisma, he said there was something about me he was very impressed with.'

So how did he fail to win over Sharon Stone?

'Steven was interested in one thing – making Steven a star. Sharon was interested in one thing – becoming a star,' said an assistant producer on the project, who requested: 'Don't name me. They're now both big shots – I've got to work in this town and between them they could finish me.' She added: 'I don't think anybody knew they were being assholes. They were just very ambitious – and assholes. The two seem to go together.'

Above the Law was an important project for Sharon Stone, in that Hollywood was paying much attention to 'Ovitz's boy'. Andrew Davis, who in 1993 would go on to direct Harrison Ford in the brilliant film adaptation of television's *The Fugitive* series, was brought in as director. Top screen-writers were hired, but, sagely, the budget was kept under $10 million. Everything is worth a gamble but, of course, you only wager so much. 'As soon as I saw Steven, I knew that, given the right vehicle, he could become a major star,' says Tony Ludwig, president of Imagine Films, adding: 'The closest person I'd ever seen carrying himself with the same stature was Mikhail Baryshnikov. Steven is smooth, powerful and has that don't-mess-with-me presence. It is almost as if he is a manufactured human being. Steven has the most amazing presence you've ever seen. When he walks into a room you can see every head – male and female – turn around as if they're all wondering who this guy is. It's sheer magnetism.'

Sharon Stone hated him; Seagal thought of her as 'just another blonde' on the film set. His role as former CIA agent Nico Toscani was what was important. Which was true. Action heroes are cash cows. Once the public adopts an action man they just keep bringing in money. The trick is to be able to package and sell them. There are scores of misfires on the action-man front, like David Carradine, who could never repeat his TV success in *Kung Fu* on the big screen, or

Jan-Michael Vincent who didn't click with the mass audience. Seagal, ploughing his way karate chop-chop through half a dozen bad guys at a time, did. He also had the advantage of looking as though he actually could think through a complex investigation rather than, like Schwarzenneger, being able only to blockade his way to a successful conclusion.

During filming on location in Chicago, Sharon Stone learned the wisdom of 'connections'. Everyone working on *Above the Law* knew that their star was associated with Michael Ovitz. One evening in the summer of 1987, at Charlie's Bar on Rush Street in Chicago, a local lawyer joined a group from the movie for drinks. 'Are you sure this movie is going to be released? Who is this guy?' he asked.

The crew were indignant. 'Hey, just wait and see,' one of them told him, adding: 'Seagal is no lightweight. One of his star students is the most powerful agent in Hollywood. No one is going to mess with this film.'

And no one did. Certainly, Seagal's confidence was important. When he went to Warner Brothers Studios they gave him a choice of scripts, he picked one but told the studios: 'The concept is great but the script is not great.' As he tells the story, the studio then said to him: 'Well, if you're so smart, why don't you fix it?' A few days later, he presented Warners with a new script, chose Andy Davis (who would be nominated for an Oscar for *The Fugitive*) as the director and then was involved in casting co-stars Sharon Stone and Pam Grier.

Seagal plays disillusioned ex-CIA man Nico Toscani who has retired after troubling times in Vietnam. There, he had learned that the CIA was involved in smuggling opium and keeping the war alive. He goes home to Chicago and wife Sharon Stone and becomes a narcotics detective. 'He gets involved in a seemingly ordinary cocaine arrest, but there are some strange curves to the narcotics investigations, even back home in America.

'My domestic life with Sharon is affected by what is going on with the cops. Nico starts climbing the ladder, and he sees that the people who are involved at the top of this cocaine thing are the same people he knew in Vietnam doing the opium. And now it's not Vietnam, it's El Salvador, Nicaragua, Guatemala. And they're funding the war down there, because war is the greatest business and that's why we always start wars. The CIA and everybody sees that he sees this and they decide to terminate him . . . Sharon and Pam and everyone else Nico has contact with is involved, is threatened.'

The impeccably-tailored, pony-tailed Seagal, whose *Under Siege* was one of the great action hits of the 1990s, says that much of the plot of *Above the Law* was based on his own experiences. But he points out: 'I wouldn't like to say that it was 100 per cent my idea, but I'm the one that has the background. An example? Well, I learned that a very high-up White House official had given the go-ahead for the assassination attempt on a United States Ambassador. I started investigating and I found out that apparently – and I can't swear for the accuracy of all my information, although I personally believe it to be totally infallible – there were a couple of major cocaine dealers that a US Ambassador in South America was going to be putting away. And the dealers told some people high up in the US Government that if they got screwed they were going to completely stop all the cocaine that was funding the Contras in Nicaragua . . . And so somebody high up in the White House apparently said: "Kill him." I'm serious about this. Andy Davis and I thought the film would never get released. I imagined the Government would confiscate it.

'It was based on fact. Everybody thought it was a simple action film, but if you listen to what's being said, there's a lot going on. When I was on tour with Sharon, I saw on national television a newscaster talking about the CIA being involved in narcotics trafficking for the purposes of funding covert operations and possibly funding the Contras which the CIA created. And that was what *Above the Law* was about. I cannot to this day believe we got away with saying what we said.

'If I taught Sharon or anyone else I've worked with anything, it's you have to travel up the escalator fighting for control of your own destiny, your own career. If you're in control, then, if you fail, you have to blame yourself, but if someone else is in control it's a hopeless feeling.'

Sharon Stone wasn't in control on *Above the Law*. Her career at the time was like a blast of buckshot – all over the place. The Seagal movie got her lots of exposure and the word was building in Hollywood that this was an actress to take notice of . . . but rumours also began spreading. Was she too much of a good-time-girl?

8

Action

'I must be legendary in bed'
– Sharon Stone, 1992

Sharon Stone is built for attention and has never had to put out any flags to be noticed. By the late 1980s, she had learned how the System worked. She knew how to play, to milk it. Mostly it was for fun, for a lark. She was chased by all the eminent Lotharios in town, including between-the-sheets legend Warren Beatty and his bedroom rival and neighbour on Los Angeles' Mulholland Drive, Jack Nicholson. Stone and her lookalike best friend, the blonde actress Mimi Craven, were a delectable duo.

They were always being approached and talked to at restaurants like the Rangoon Racquet Club, The Grill, The Ivy and Tribeca in Beverly Hills. On Sunset Strip they would often have dinner at Wolfgang Puck's Spago. 'Sharon loved to make an entrance. She'd have a champagne cocktail at the bar and, like everybody else, wait for a table. After *Basic Instinct*, the champagne cocktail was waiting at her table,' said a former Spago waiter who, like almost everyone in Hollywood, is now a screenwriter.

Chuck Binder was getting Stone lots of auditions for middling movies and high-profile cable and regular television films. However, she has never denied indulging in her own high-flying exploits. She was once detained by customs officers in Tokyo, who suspected her of smuggling Cartier watches and cash. She and a European designer, who she has never named, were both strip-searched by Japanese officials. The authorities said they were working on 'inside information' in their investigation. And there was the rich film producer she allowed to fly her to Paris on Concorde – in return for bringing her home with suitcases packed with the latest fashions. Of this story, she does her pussycat act, saying: 'I *do* know how to travel with only a change of G-strings, a passport, something black and an attitude.'

With success comes the sniping. After the box-office landslide of *Basic Instinct*, everyone in Hollywood had a Sharon Stone story. As with Madonna and her overwhelming success, many people had bad and raunchy stories to tell and sell. There were stories of drug-taking and nymphomania. But, of course, anyone who had seen *Basic Instinct* could have conjured up where these tales were created. Stone does not offer herself as some squeaky-clean lady and it's not the drug-taking or sex allegations that upset her.

'What pisses me off is all this stuff about not being able to act. That I was some blonde who just got lucky. Honey, I *worked* for all that I got. For years, directors had been telling me: "Baby, you're the next Jessica Lange." Also, for years, I'd been testing for parts with a star. The director would want me, the star would want me, then I'd be on hold for ten to fourteen days while, if they could get a bigger name star, I wouldn't get the part. Three times, I've had the leading man call me during production and say: "I just want you to know I still wish it was you." Not because the actress wasn't any good but because we had a particular rapport. I was doing good work in not so good movies. Over the years I'd been devoted to training, studying and working. You're not going to go for brain surgery from somebody who just got their bachelor's degree. You train, learn and grow and it's natural that you move into that group of people who are doing the same thing. I *earned* my way into that club.

'From the day I got *Basic Instinct* I heard all the rumours. The drugs one was new to me! I'd just like to know how I could be on drugs and make four movies a year, because in those days I would have been doing that. I'm sure making *Police Academy 4* would have been a lot funnier on drugs . . . When I heard that I was supposedly really promiscuous, I said to my boyfriend: "Honey, I'm a traaaaammmmpppppppp. Let's just do it on the hood of the car – make me live up to my reputation tonight." He didn't think it was funny, but I do.

'When I did *Year of the Gun*, I heard I was sleeping with John Frankenheimer. When I was tested for *Basic Instinct*, I was sleeping with Paul Verhoeven and having an affair with Michael Douglas. I must be legendary in bed. Guess it must be the drugs, huh?'

Stone has never lost her sense of humour over all the allegations that have followed her stardom. In fact, they amuse her and she pins the more outrageous allegations about her life – especially the sexual ones – on a heart-shaped billboard she calls 'Cupid'.

'Because I obviously don't know as many people as some people say, lots of stuff gets made up about what I have or haven't done. Some of the stuff that was made up I wish I *had* done – some of it is hurtful and mean. It's come back to me that I've been with a lot of guys, some that I don't even know, some that I have been on dates with.

'Some people have also told me that I'm gay. If you are a woman finding any degree of success, that you could have possibly earned it by professionalism and integrity seems to have escaped the "minds" in this Hollywood environment . . . That you fucked your way to the top seems to be a more palatable concept. I never thought I was sexy, I don't think anybody else ever thought I was, so, if suddenly people think I'm sexy, that's good. But when they start saying I got my job by fucking somebody I want to just flatten them.'

She and her friend Mimi Craven went to On The Rox, a nightclub on Sunset Boulevard where Beverly Hills ends and the Sunset Strip begins. It is an exclusive place and enjoys the attention of present and former roués like Jack Nicholson, Warren Beatty and other familiar-faced gadabouts.

Nicholson, who has a penchant for blondes – especially staggeringly-shaped wise-cracking ones – was smitten. Immediately. But Stone played a waiting game. It got her an invitation to Warren Beatty's home, an electronically-guarded Colditz a moment's drive away from the compound shared by Nicholson and Marlon Brando, on what is known as Casanova Corner on Mulholland Drive, which links the sub-urban San Fernando Valley with Beverly Hills and downtown Los Angeles.

Stone uses long words when she talks about Beatty. How did they meet? 'One of his friends was pursuant of me and I didn't respond.'

What happened? 'Warren called my agent about having a meeting with me – at his house – about some project. I told my agent Paula Kramer: "I'm not going to Warren Beatty's house by myself." She said: "Oh, good, I want to go too." So we gals went up for a half-hour meeting over tea that lasted almost three hours. He's a bright, interesting, occasionally fascinating man, and it's a crime that he doesn't go on screen and play a character full of life, information, savvy and wonder. It turned out all the meeting was about was he wanted to know why I hadn't called his friend back. That helped me learn a little more about living in Hollywood.'

Did she get involved with Jack Nicholson? She replied: 'Ask Jack.' Nicholson's agent said: 'We never comment on anything other than his acting assignments.'

But in Hollywood it was certainly rumoured that the couple had a short but passionate affair. Interestingly, Stone has never been a kiss and tell model/starlet/star. She has always played the dating game close to her ample chest. And Nicholson doesn't brag about his many conquests – he enjoys them.

William Stadiem is the co-author of *Madam 90210*, which is

the 1990s Bible of the sexual peccadilloes of Tinseltown. It was an 1994 American best-seller, which he wrote with the total co-operation of Beverly Hills Madam Alex Adams. He had heard the rumours about Sharon Stone and confirmed one of them: 'Yes, a producer took her – she was then a starlet but now is a huge star – to Paris and he was praising about her at the end of the trip. But it was the most expensive trip he'd ever taken because, not only did he have to give her money for the trip, he had to buy her a fortune in finery. Otherwise she would get depressed and would pout. Oh, he said, she would pout. Even though he had paid for her company, it wasn't very good company unless she was dressing in the style she wanted to be accustomed to. It was a very, very expensive week. But he seemed, finally, to believe it was very, very much worth it.'

Stadiem says his book – and research – was into the ultimate guilty pleasure for men who have everything – sex with the women of their dreams. And, if they desire, different dreams or kinks every night or day or lunchtime or teatime. *Anytime.* They can have whatever style of women or sex they want and pick their lusts from the pages of *Vogue* or *Harper's Bazaar* or the latest television show or cinema blockbuster. Women will literally walk off the pages of the glossy fashion magazines or entertainment screens and into bed with men willing to pay. And female lawyers and accountants and doctors and dentists can happily be lured into selling sex because of the money available. In Hollywood there is a price for everything. And, seemingly, everyone.

Tinseltown sells sex. But it also buys it. Lots of it. Every second of the day. And the men buying are rich and famous, powerful and celebrated.

Author William Stadiem is a little amused by the shocked faces when people learn that their favourite actor buys sex. He argues that they pay for everything else from Lear jets to dog psychologists, so what's different? A great deal, of course. But Stadiem, a Truman Capote type of figure, is more interested in the what and the why and with whom, than the morality, for he says: 'High-level prostitution is Hollywood's best-kept dirty secret.'

It is the subtleties of the game which are fascinating and intriguing. The customer who runs up an annual $1 million tab for girls. The cross-dressing and premature ejaculations of famous names – name dropping really. The OPEC minister who has a 'regular', a six-foot-tall former ballet dancer; the sexaholic producer who never sees a girl twice; the CPA (Chartered Public Accountant) who loves sex and wants to work as a hooker to make money and meet interesting people – she's flown first-class from Los Angeles to spend time at New York's Carlyle Hotel with a major British chief executive officer. And the hookers who have become wives to major stars and power figures in Hollywood and famous film and TV stars themselves.

But always the why, why, why? Why do men who have everything and, in the vernacular, can have anything, pay?

Bill Stadiem offers the answers in his book *Madam 90210*. It is a tale of stars and sex and, appropriately, vice versa. He was researching a business book about a Hollywood studio takeover, but found most people were reluctant to talk about dirty money. Dirty secrets were an altogether different matter. He says of his book: 'It's about sex and power in Hollywood, told from the point of view of Madam Alex Adams, who was the Madam to the stars. She's retired now, but through her I was able to interview about a hundred of the most beautiful call-girls in the world and many of their clients. In Hollywood it's a status symbol to even have been on Alex's list of customers. It was a very exclusive list, you had to have really, really arrived. It was the equivalent of a good table at Spago. I mean, to be at Alex's you knew you were a player one of the big players. The men were very proud that they could have – and talk about – all the now famous women or covergirls they had had. It was great fun. They talked to me about it. They weren't ashamed.

'Alex was just another way for these powerful and rich

men to meet the women they wanted. They liked to challenge themselves and put their egos on the line. They didn't mind paying a few thousand dollars to meet the woman for the first time. Then, the challenge was – can I get this girl to sleep with me for free the next time? It was a game.'

And an expensive game for one Beverly Hills billionaire: 'One of the former call-girls married this incredibly wealthy man, but even after they were married she demanded two million dollars for fifty acts of sex. It was very much a quota system – she still wanted to get paid for her services. He paid her. It was so good, he couldn't resist it.'

Stadiem says he has learned the power of beauty. For it is not just the sex act, it's being able to *get* the fantasy girl of their choice: 'It's the sheer excitement of being in bed with these women. These are women that you would see in magazines like *Vogue* or on TV. Men would often call Alex and say, "I saw this girl – can you get me her?" And she could do it. She had an amazing network and for "X" thousands of dollars you could have an affair with this girl. Alex's price started at one thousand dollars for an hour of pleasure and then two thousand dollars for an extended afternoon. For a whole night, it could be five thousand dollars. And if they went on trips, then the cost was more.

'The first-class sections of British Airways and Air France were frequently populated with a number of Alex's creatures. If they were starlets or models and someone spotted them, they would say they were going on a photo-shoot in Milan, but it was something else in London or Milan or wherever.

'A lot of the men pay by cash. It's a cash business. Although some of the clients of Alex and her successors run up huge tabs – it's not surprising for people to have six-digit tabs. They run up bills just the way they would at Armani or Mortons and pay it off at the end of the month. I mean these people are good for the money. What are they getting for it?

'It's very conventional sex – very normal, nothing particularly kinky. Its not so much the idea that you want to tie the

girl up or degrade her or something like that – it was the idea
of having her, having someone who you never thought you
could have, that's the excitement. It's fucking the unfuckable.

'That's one of the reasons a rich man, a handsome man, a
movie star, a man who theoretically could have anybody in
the world, would pay for sex. He would go to Alex or one of
the Madams who have replaced her and say: "Find me this
incredible creature. I want to have sex with her."

'This is the same creature this man might meet in a bar and
be able to go home for free with. But in the age of AIDS, men,
even if they are famous, cannot expect to go to a bar and pick
somebody out and go to bed with them that night.

'This is a town where time is money. People don't want to
waste a lot of time in courtship, in pursuing women that basically all they really want to do is have sex with and probably
never see again. Why should they waste their time? And the
watchwords for Hollywood in the 1990s are "family values".
These same men have families and they don't want to get
caught out having an affair with some teenage model or young
starlet. That would just defeat everything. Their box-office
depends on their image. To paraphrase that old deodorant
commercial: the Madams take the worry out of being close.

'These men can meet the most beautiful women in the
world and have sex with them, any kind of sex they want,
within reason, and pay a lot of money. But they've got a lot of
money. When somebody is making a million dollars a year, to
pay a few thousand dollars for an hour of sex with some
dream girl is a relative drop in the bucket. I met clients – so
called "power johns" – who spent more than one million
dollars a year on call-girls.

'It's amazing that people would spend so much money, but
when they have an income of twenty million dollars a year, a
million dollars a year for recreation is a drop in a gilded
bucket.

'There are no bargains in sex. They are not wanted. The
more they pay, the better they feel. It's like going to an élite

French restaurant. They feel that it's safer, it's more glamorous, it's a higher-tone experience . . . People don't look for bargains when it comes to sex. They want to pay as much as they possibly can because they feel that if they pay more they're getting more.

'You know, Tom Cruise and Julia Roberts get ten million dollars a picture and because of that, people think they are seeing a bigger picture and a bigger star. It's the same thing when the same people who are making these big movies want to hire call-girls. They want to pay more. The more people pay in Hollywood, the better they feel. They feel more secure that they're really getting quality.'

Providing 'entertainment' for stars and executives in Hollywood has long been accepted. Producer Wilbur Stark – father of Prince Andrew's one-time love Koo Stark – said that when he was a bachelor he was asked to 'arrange' girls: 'Married friends – top executives – would say: "Willy, you're single, set up a date for us." I was amazed. So I had a list of prostitutes they would call, and afterwards the girls gave me the story.'

Stadiem acknowledges the longtime 'perk' of Hollywood success. 'This is the golden triangle of sex in America, the most expensive neighbourhood in the world. Houses on the small lots start at three million dollars.'

Up Rodeo Drive and into the Hollywood Hills, the $1.6 million ranch-style home of Heidi Fleiss is not much compared to others in Benedict Canyon. But it's not drab for a high-school drop-out who moved in on Madam Alex's territory when the former queen of the game was busted and placed on probation.

'Heidiwood' was the Hollywood scandal of the summer of 1993. It may have scandalised the rest of the world, but having a twenty-seven-year-old woman supplying movie stars, male and female, and film studio executives and captains of industry with the most stunning women you will ever see is shrugged off in the town where it happens.

When you can buy anything you want, why not? So does Stadiem believe almost any woman in Hollywood is for sale?

'I wouldn't say that. I think a lot of men would like to think that, and perhaps everybody has her price at some point. I'd say that a lot of young and ambitious women, women under twenty-five, could use extra money. Unless they had made it in the movies by that age they, you know, could always use more money.

'Alex was a florist in town and in the course of that business she met her predecessor, an Englishwoman, who decided to get out of sex and become a dog breeder. She told Alex she wanted to sell her her black book. Alex hesitated and the Englishwoman told her: "You were in flowers, now you can be in deflowers."

'Alex became probably the world's most important Madam with movie stars and major politicians and statesmen and some of the biggest moguls in the world from America and Europe. She's had them all – it's one of the great luxury items. If anybody has the money, they kind of want to try it out of curiosity.

'It's very, very civilised. It's like a dating service except the dates will cost you a thousand dollars and upwards. But for men who are not price-sensitive that doesn't mean anything.

'These girls are charming. They're from all over the world. I've met lawyers, accountants, development girls from the studios, and they find it an amazing way to make a lot of money in a very short time. And even though we are living in an age of caution today, these are children from the sixties. When you walk around Beverly Hills you see beautiful women in the street who look very Grace Kelly and refined, but these people know what the world is about. And to spend a hour or several hours with a man, and make thousands of dollars for that, can buy a lot of nice clothes and a lot of apartments in Beverly Hills which is the most materialistic place on earth. It's hard to resist the need, the desire to have as much money as you possibly can.

'Some of the girls have married very well and become Hollywood Wives. Others have become Hollywood producers or executives. A large number have become actresses, starlets, models. And a lot of the models, when their modelling careers are over and they are too wooden to act, manage to marry very rich and prominent men.

'In Beverly Hills and Hollywood, superficial is fine. If a woman is beautiful that's enough, yet that's why you see so many ugly divorces here. After a while, a lot of these women let their mercenary roots show and the men who marry them are not cured of their sexaholism by marrying perfect call-girl types. They find themselves calling the Madams again. It's a hard habit to break. They're often busted by becoming patrons of younger call-girls and their ex-call-girl wives catch them. Nobody can smell a call-girl like a former call-girl. Sherlock Holmes is not a better sleuth at sniffing out a husband's commercial indiscretions.'

Marriage or fame can change outlook, as Stadiem notes, quoting Marilyn Monroe's famous line, when she finally became a star: 'I'll never have to suck another cock in this town again'.

Stadiem talks of another starlet, now a famous name, who cost one Hollywood producer tens of thousands of dollars. 'She's a huge star now, one of the biggest. A number of girls have become huge TV and movie stars. You can turn the TV on anytime and see them, and a lot of them have become very prominent social housewives. They've become ladies who lunch.

'It was a brief window of opportunity in their path. One didn't have to be a call-girl for a long time to make wonderful contacts. They become trophy girlfriends, trophy call-girls, trophy wives. It's just trophydom continued. . .

'When a woman marries a famous man in Hollywood she is immediately accepted in Beverly Hills. Money talks. Power talks. This is a town where knowledge is knowledge and power is power. Power really derives from money here, and if a call-girl marries a rich and powerful man her past is accept-able and forgiven. In Hollywood, having been a call-girl is a market status because it meant you were one of the most beautiful and one of the best . . . Blue-stockings may sneer at it. But this is not a town of blue-stockings, is it? . . . This is a town of meshed stockings.'

'If you want anything, just whistle,' Lauren Bacall purred to Humphrey Bogart in her debut film. She was sultry and sexy, but revealed nothing but her dental work in 1944's *To Have and Have Not*. She was nineteen, and her act seduced audi-ences and Bogart, who married her.

In 1994, just a shade short of fifty years later, actresses are still trying to turn audiences on, but are, well, rather more forward. After *Basic Instinct* and the stunning success it pro-vided for Sharon Stone, scripts in Hollywood included dozens of pages of material reflecting naked ambition for box-office hits.

Lauren Bacall believes one pair of knickers too many has been dropped, and prefers the style of yesteryear: 'Glamour was great, it was total glamour in the movies and it was so seductive you just wanted to be part of it. It had such an aura, and now it's kind of too graphic. Everyone knows everything about how movies are made, what goes on, how special effects are done and who wears what and who's doing it to who. I don't know . . . I don't know . . . It's just too explicit in every direction. The great thing about what we now call "old movies" is that you were able to use your imagination. You were able to envision whatever you wanted, whatever you were able to imagine instead of having it all laid out in front of you.

'I think romance is almost a thing of the past as far as movies are concerned. I think it's sad, because I think romance is something people always want and look for. It's what you hope for, what takes you out of your reality.

'I think the sex thing – I mean, I like sex as much as anyone but don't wanna watch it on television or on the screen in a movie theatre. I don't want to watch Michael Douglas at it all the time, thank you. I really don't, cute as he is.' Bacall warms to her theme: 'Julia Roberts – she's only twenty-years old or something and she's making a comeback. I mean, that's pretty stupid, isn't it? Sharon Stone, who came from nowhere, right, and she's been around, as it turns out, but it's always one break that makes the difference. She's made a noise and she's got kind of an old-time movie star look about her which is great. There's always a place for that, but who knows how long any of these women are gonna last if it's only based on a small thing.

'Madonna certainly was one person who made a wave, but I think she was different because she was really so smart about selling herself in such a major way that she's become almost a world unto herself. You can't call her a flash in the pan because she's been around too long. For actresses, you can't just shoot your wad the first time out – you have to have some talent that's going to last.

'When I went out to California I was eighteen and I didn't know anything about anything. Bette Davis was the big star – she owned the Warner Brothers lot. Barbara Stanwyck and Ann Sheridan – they were the top ones. And you had Garbo and Katharine Hepburn and Lana Turner, Ava Gardner, Norma Shearer and Joan Crawford. I mean, endless women stars.'

But, unlike Sharon Stone, stars without power. Bacall agrees that men did and do run Hollywood: 'It's still a chauvinistic town. Women have to struggle and fight. The sex and violence – I don't blame television to some degree for doing that obvious kind of cheap stuff. It's not quality time that is spent watching these shows . . . I think if women were more in control the stuff would be better.'

But, she admits, women have never been in control. She's asked about sexual harassment in Hollywood. She clearly doesn't regard it as some new politically incorrect art form: 'That's always existed at any business at any office. The casting couch theory was always true for people in the theatre, in the movies. Lots of executives have their girlfriends in movies. If they're lousy they don't last very long.'

Actress Theresa Russell, a friend of Sharon Stone and Madonna, has no illusions: 'There is no doubt about the business of sex for movie roles. Definitely, the casting couch does exist. There are a lot of women who will unfortunately pretty much do anything in order to get their foot in the door. That's the nature of it. If you haven't got talent, you get found out pretty quick. It's just there is so much competition. Say they have Mel Gibson to do a film, and they go through a list to find a female lead. If it's not Kim Basinger then maybe it's Michelle Pfeiffer. If it's not Michelle Pfeiffer, maybe it's somebody else – the women are completely interchangeable and it's sort of cast on who thinks she's fanciable. It's true, it really happens.

'Women get taken advantage of. They really do. Even ones who are sort of semi-established. I did some work with Molly Ringwald and I had a lot of conversations with her. You go into a slump and people want you to do all this stuff, come in for readings and wear a bathing suit so they can see what your body looks like. In her time, after she'd proved herself, that happened to her here. I wouldn't do it, and I think they'd be scared to ask me. I'd say no and tell them to shove it where the light never goes. I'm not that desperate. The world does not revolve for me around this town.'

Sex sells and Hollywood has been marketing it since the silent days. Russ Meyer, the producer of super-mammary films like *Beyond the Valley of the Dolls* and *Faster, Pussy Cat* is a master purveyor. 'The girls in my films, if they wanted to work in the major studios, were always told that the casting couch must be a consideration. I won't mention names, but big-time guys, some of the most unpleasant men I've ever met, are major film producers.

'I've often said that X-rated film-makers don't have to have a couch, it comes to them real easy, but the casting agents, producers, directors often try to extract the . . . er, flesh as well. I'm not saying all of them are like this, but I've been led to believe by a lot of women that it happens regularly. I don't audition people for the sake of acquiring some kind of sexual relief. I'm there to make a film.'

Phyllis Diller, who has been in Hollywood for more than fifty years, says: 'The casting couch is the name of the game in Hollywood. It goes on all the time. I like to think that the people who become really big stars are very bright and very talented and worked hard. That's what I like to think. However, I know there are stars, especially women, who have made a career from sexual favours.'

Britain's Helen Mirren, who had to endure her own Hollywood upset over the casting of the big screen *Prime Suspect*, is tough talking about sex on- and off-screen and the domino effect.

'The film industry has always had this loose kind of thing going on . . . a sort of *laissez faire* liberality. Obviously, there's room for improvement, but I would hate to see my profession become very structured and full of you must do this, you mustn't do that. You know what's offensive and what isn't. Sexual harassment has very little to do with sex. It's more to do with power and domination. It's saying I can do what I like to you and you can't do anything about it.

'Sexual harassment has always gone on in Hollywood. Absolutely. It was a joke, wasn't it, really, the old casting couch or whatever? I always thought it was a joke and now women are saying, well, actually guys, it wasn't a joke. Actually, no, we never found it very funny. Actually, it really pissed us off. And we're going to get our own back.'

She is concerned by the image being given, the message being transmitted, in some films today. One, in particular, angers her: Sharon Stone's arch-rival Julia Roberts' *Pretty Woman*: 'It was so immoral. I couldn't believe it. It was just so horribly and I think immorally and unspeakably disgusting and misleading. I live in Hollywood and I know what

Hollywood hookers look like. And I know what Hollywood Boulevard is. America's full of people who don't live the glamorous life that's constantly show on television and in films and I think of a fourteen-year-old girl in Waco, Texas, seeing that film

'I know what I was like when I was fourteen, those images are terribly seductive, you believe in your dream world that that could happen. That's not what happens. That's not what Hollywood hookers are like. Their lives are horrendous. I'm sure that there were many little girls who thought, I know how to get rich and marry a millionaire, by going to suck dicks on Hollywood Boulevard. That was a truly violent film because I'm sure that film was responsible for destroying quite a lot of lives.'

Sharon Stone was getting on with her life. She was making good film connections. Producer Joel Silver – the man responsible for the majority of film mayhem in the 1980s including Mel Gibson's *Lethal Weapon* series and Bruce Willis' *Die Hard* movies – cast her in *Action Jackson*. This was to be another money-making franchise cashing in on the popularity of Carl Weathers, who had spent a decade playing Sylvester Stallone's boxing opponent and then friend and trainer Apollo Creed in four *Rocky* films. A former American-football player, the 6ft 2ins-tall Weathers was cast as Jerico 'Action' Jackson, a larger-than-life lawyer-turned-cop on the streets of Detroit. The statuesque Vanity provided the curves on the good guy side, while Craig T. Nelson was the car tycoon villain, with Stone helping him indulge his nastiness.

'I struggled a pretty long time at the beginning of it, trying to figure out what role I might have in the entertainment industry,' says Weathers, adding: 'It would have been easy to put it in cruise control and let everyone else take care of everything – a lot of people have done that. But I would have gone crazy that way. I'm a little bit of a control freak. I've got to have *my hands* in the pie. That's something Sharon understood.

I had my own company [Stormy Weather Productions] when we were making *Action Jackson*, and I think she realised then that unless you have some control in your career you're the one being controlled.'

Weathers, like Stone, has worked with both Sylvester Stallone and Arnold Schwarzenegger, and says he learned discipline from them. 'From Sharon I learned patience – and that you just keep working. There was never any doubt in my mind that one day she was going to be in the major league.'

9

Total Babe

'Everybody enjoys the power of sexuality'
– Sharon Stone, 1991

It was a year after she had made *Action Jackson* that Sharon Stone was working on a film in New York. 'I leaped, totally freaked out, from a cab that had just rear-ended the cab in front of it. I was screaming: "Did you see what that stupid idiot did?" And some guy says: "Weren't you the girl in *Action Jackson*?"'

Ah, fame! But only a touch of the attention that was coming her way.

Sharon Stone was going to take her clothes off. And put some muscle on herself – and Arnold Schwarzenegger. Disenchanted with what seemed to be her terminal role as 'the beautiful blonde' – and how long was that going to last? – Stone made several trips back to Pennsylvania, to her 'roots', while she tried to decide whether to stay in the acting game. Yes, there were films. She made *Tears in the Rain* for America's Showtime cable network: 'I played a beautiful blonde in a soppy romance, and I got such vicious, scathing reviews that lots of big stars, producers and directors sent me consoling letters, flowers and gifts. In 1989 I made *Blood and Sand*, and I played a beautiful blonde in a role that did wonders for Rita Hayworth [in 1941] but did considerably less for me.'

She also played a nasty, vindictive 'beautiful blonde – a rehearsal of sorts for *Basic Instinct* – in *He Said, She Said* in 1991, as well as appearing with Forrest Whitaker in *Diary of a Hit Man* and with Andrew McCarthy in John '*The Manchurian Candidate*' Frankenheimer's *Year of the Gun*.

Sharon Stone was working. But was anybody noticing? Just some of the biggest players in Hollywood.

Arnold Schwarzenegger had, like Sharon Stone, spent the 1980s working towards becoming a major star. His sixteen-stone of bodyfatless beefcake, this walking-around Mount Gorgeous, didn't even hint MENSA. But he and Stone both had good minds as well as perfectly developed bodies. Schwarzenegger, because of his bulk and grand sense of self-promotion, got much more notice as he worked his way towards becoming Mr Hollywood. There was a steady stream of films, *Conan the Barbarian* (1982), *Conan the Destroyer* (1984), *The Terminator* (1984), *Commando* (1985), *Raw Deal* (1986), *Predator* (1987), *The Running Man* (1987) and *Twins* in 1988. That movie, with the idea of the big man and tiny Danny DeVito cast in the title role, made you laugh. It also pleased everybody involved as a box-office smash – it made more than $20 million on opening day in America, and Schwarzenegger could name his price.

And his movie. And director. And co-star. And location. The man with a name like a cavalry charge had broken the box-office barrier. Which was good news for Sharon Stone. She was about to be involved in state-of-the-art film-making, and learn what being a star can be all about.

Which is being in control, being the boss.

Making *Total Recall* saw Schwarzenegger also take on the role of commander-in-chief, for making the film was like making war. It cost $70 million, required armies of stuntmen, arsenals of advanced weapons and barrels and barrels of fake blood. It was a logistical leviathan that took up ten giant soundstages at the Churubusco Studios in Mexico City. In what seemed like an ongoing airlift, advanced equipment was ferried in from the special effects centres in Hollywood and George '*Star Wars*' Lucas' Industrial Light and Magic headquarters in Marin County in northern California.

Sharon Stone and everyone else involved were about to learn what moviemaking of the future would entail. She had been sent the script with a memo reading: 'We're interested in meeting you for this action movie.'

She recalls being disdainful about another 'action' film: 'I was quite angry and said: "I've done every stupid action movie I'm going to do. No, thank you!" Then they told me that Paul Verhoeven was directing it and I said: "Oh, OK. I don't need to go to a meeting. If they want me, I'll do it."

'I had seen his films and thought they were terrific. Then I met him and was completely enamoured of him. I was cast.' And fate was sealed. But only just. As with much of Sharon Stone's life, it was happenstance waiting to happen.

Total Recall was based on the story *We Can Remember It For You Wholesale*, by the late and legendary science-fiction writer Philip K. Dick. The first script was written in 1974 by Dan O'Bannon and Ronald Shusett, who would later write the original Sigourney Weaver success *Alien*.

For the next fifteen years, the complex story of a twenty-first century construction worker, who must find his stolen memory in a rebellious mining colony on Mars, went through Hollywood hell. It was constantly rewritten. Directors including Fred Schepisi (*Roxanne* and *The Russia House*) and Bruce Beresford (*Driving Miss Daisy*) and David Cronenberg (*The Fly*) failed to get it into production.

The wily Schwarzenegger believed he knew the reason. Italian film tycoon Dino de Laurentiis (who told everyone he ever met: 'I can make you a star') who had owned the rights to *Total Recall* for half a dozen years could not stop haemorrhaging money, never mind raising the tens of millions of dollars to make the first big action movies of the 1990s.

Schwarzenegger had worked for de Laurentiis – playing Conan the Barbarian and Conan the Destroyer in 1982 and

1984 – but the two men could not agree on what to do about *Total Recall*. The big man adored the project, but played poker with it. He sensed that the Italian producer was in trouble with his Churubusco Studios and other enterprises. De Laurentiis went bankrupt and, in 1988, had a sale of properties to raise funds. Schwarzenegger persuaded Carolco Pictures – then, ironically, riding the success of Sylvester Stallone's *Rambo* films – to buy the Mexico City studios for him.

'Arnold single-handedly made this happen,' says co-screenwriter Ronald Shusett, who shares a producer credit on the film with Buzz Feitshans who worked on the three *Rambo* films. 'By the time it did happen, I couldn't believe it. I'd given up in despair. But Arnold and Paul Verhoeven just rammed it right through, because they are so formidable and worth taking a chance on.'

Schwarzenegger says he always wanted the director of *Total Recall* to be a mix of philosopher and visual stylist as well as miracle worker in the logistics department. He saw *Robocop* time and time again, and also Verhoeven's first English language feature, the sex and swordplay epic *Flesh and Blood*, which was made in 1985, and, of course, his classics like *The Fourth Man* and *Soldier of Orange*. And he wanted the Dutch director. Again he persuaded Carolco Pictures to grant his wishes.

Verhoeven regards himself as a man of vision and sometimes it is a vision that only someone with a warped mind could imagine. The graphic violence in *Total Recall* and, later, in *Basic Instinct* had to be toned down to get mainstream cinema release ratings. But down in Mexico City, Sharon Stone and her co-stars like Rachel Ticotin, Michael Ironside and Ronny Cox were in for a new experience.

The Dutchman does not employ what you would call subdued working methods. He blocks shots, but he also plays out every actor's role along with those of the cameramen – shouting at the top of his voice.

During production, he uses up several temper tantrums a

day – during the making of *Basic Instinct* he received three bleeding noses, one from Stone and two from Michael Douglas – and often is the cliché of the mad genius. He's a perfectionist who will do everything he can to get what he wants. He laughs at this.

'If you're making a movie for $60 million – which is what these movies can cost – at least you should try to assure yourself that you're making it in a way that will bring the money back.

'It is dangerous and uneconomic to shoot a mutilated script. I mean, the movie can be as artistic a statement as you can make it, but it should be an economic statement too. So you agree to deliver a movie that, in your opinion, will make the money back. Then they come along and say: "Take these scenes out!" Well, the movie won't work and that's when I get really angry and fight for the script.'

That, of course, is music to the ears of someone like Arnold Schwarzenegger, who doesn't simply want to be a popular cultural icon but a financially successful icon.

Producer Buzz Feitshans says that he and Verhoeven had daily confrontations over the budget and then added: 'Make that hourly. We fought a lot. There was a lot of screaming and yelling and ranting and raving. As in most things it always came down to "I'll give you two of these and I'll take four of those". Arnold was involved in the discussions and in many cases he was the mediator . . . The players like Sharon and Ronny Cox hadn't seen anything like it. We were there to make a twenty-first century movie – and we made it. That's the miracle.'

Sharon Stone had to convince Schwarzenegger that she could play his wife, a woman who is really part of the conspiracy to steal his character's mind. On the film set in Mexico City, members of the crew and cast said they believed the big muscle man was intimidated by Stone, who in the film plays a memorably malicious minx who kicks and punches with tremendous fury.

She remembers: 'I definitely had to prove my chops to *earn* Arnold's respect. It was tough and I did it – that's why I liked this part. I'd made nearly twenty films, been in the biggest television mini-series ever made and more than sixty TV commercials and people would still say: "Don't I know you?" This made the difference. It was a Western for the 1990s – violent, way over the top, but you're laughing.'

Eventually, everybody was.

Schwarzenegger really performed as the boss. 'He showed us what could be done,' says Sharon Stone adding: 'I'm not saying you had to love Arnold but you could admire him for what he achieved.'

He is sometimes blunt in his ways. And vulgar. He teased one Mexican extra on *Total Recall* about the alignment of her breasts, he woke up Ronald Shusett from an afternoon siesta by drenching the screenwriter-producer's crotch in iced water.

'I knew from Africa that on these long location films – and *Total Recall* was twenty weeks – that you've got to know when to make a joke and when to take a joke,' said Sharon Stone.

Schwarzenegger, wandering down the corridor of the Four Seasons Hotel in Beverly Hills, is in an inspired mood. He has just predicted the first weekend earnings of half a dozen new films. In his hotel suite he learns he was on the button. As he was with *Total Recall*. 'It was a difficult film to make but everyone learned from it. Sharon Stone was perfect in the role and I believe that was because we all worked so hard at it – Sharon, Paul and myself. Sharon knew there were no shortcuts. She had to look the part and *be* the part. I think that's the big lesson she learned from the movie. There were so many things going on that everyone had to pull their weight.'

Regarded as a joke in Hollywood in his body-building days, the muscle man proved the success of mind over matter – and vice versa – to Stone.

Before *Total Recall* even opened in cinemas in America it was a word-of-mouth success. By then, Schwarzenegger's movies had earned more than $1 billion. They said that not since Jean Harlow had a body been able to smash and grab such box-office revenue. Stone regarded all this with amazement – at first. Schwarzenegger had co-starred with dragons, grunted out sentences of six words or less in a funny accent and was big and brawny – and bankable.

But it takes effort. And vision. Paul Verhoeven said: 'If it was only action I would have been bored. It's psychological, it's about schizophrenia. What's real. What's not real. That's what interested me.'

So, for six months they filmed in Mexico City, using eight sound stages, forty-five separate sets, one hundred computerised bluescreen shots, robot-driven cars, holographic chases and enough action sequences to have loaned out a few to that year's other action movies like *Dick Tracy* and *Die Hard*.

Schwarzenegger's character Quaid wanders through a neon-lit world of psychic parlours, porno shops, brothels and bars. There's what looks like a fast-food shop but then the sign, in focus, reads: 'Plastic surgery while you wait'. There are evil forces at work and the pollution equals a smoggy day in Los Angeles in July. People have been turned into mutants. Some walk around with their brains growing outside their skulls. A taxi driver has a wing under his arm. A prostitute shows off her three perfect breasts. And there are the Arnie-isms. 'Look who's talking,' he says to a deformed alien who says to him: 'You got a nerve showing your face around here.' Or 'Screw you!' to a bad guy at the wrong end of Arnie's drill.

It was not Shakespeare, but then, we are not talking Olivier – this was the biggest action star in the world, who had torn, trampled, punched, shot and fought his way like a one-man catastrophe through the sword and sorcery *Conans*, the automatic fire of contemporary mayhem and then was good enough not to allow that acting felon Danny DeVito to steal all the laughs in *Twins*.

Sharon Stone watched. And learned.

'Arnold is the biggest baby you'll ever meet. He's just a big, big baby. But he wants you to do the best you can because he wants his team to win. It's not an individual sport for Arnold. Arnold is a Movie Star. I made fun of him right off the bat. We were doing rehearsals in a hotel room. Arnold was lying on the bed and Paul Verhoeven was on top of him, straddling him, caressing his hair, explaining to me how he thought the scene ought to go. I said: "I think I'll leave you two guys alone. You're so darn cute together!"

'Arnold is unbelievably focused and available. He tries harder than most people I've worked with. So I worked out for two months. I did circuit training, I did karate – I didn't want to die. I'd do the Life-cycle for half an hour and then the weight machines from one to the next. I'd move, move, move for three hours. Then I'd finish with sit-ups and stretching. I worked my buns off. As I said, I was doing karate, but I'd always studied *tae kwondo*, so I was moderately familiar with the martial arts. While we were filming I worked out at the hotel in Mexico City.

'I'd work out until guys would puke and then I would stop. It was kind of a macho thing for me. Before it was over I was big. I was buff. I could kick some ass. The fight scenes with Arnold were exhausting but they were a blast.

'The bedroom scenes? The *Total Recall* scenes were about manipulation, about gaining power over Arnold by being sexual.

'It wasn't really a "sex" scene. I had a nightgown on! And Arnold wore briefs. It wasn't like *Basic Instinct* which dealt with a very weird, very sick sort of love. In *Total Recall* Arnold has his briefs on!'

In the film, Stone, as the kick-boxing, manipulative wife, gives Schwarzenegger some physical stick. 'What was it like to kick Arnold Schwarzenegger's butt? It was great. I got a wonderful response from women. They told their boyfriends: "I'm going to do that to you." Let's be honest, we're all pissed off about something.'

Make-up and special effects wizard Rob Bottin – the designer on *Robocop* – constructed a complicated, computer-controlled puppet for the Martian mutant leader and it got plugged into the wrong power source. Another major problem was the Martian-colony film sets, huge constructions that could hold more than one hundred people. Most of them incorporated enormous windows that looked out on elaborate vistas of Mars. In reality these 'windows' were forty-foot by sixty-foot bluescreen backdrops, against which models of the Mars landscape were projected in post-production. No one had ever shot such big bluescreens behind film sets before and the meticulous lighting that bluescreening demands took almost a day per shot to rig, slowing production down .

And there were the injuries on the film, the highest screen body-count since Verhoeven's *Robocop*. Rachel Ticotin, who played Schwarzenegger's long-lost love, the guerrilla Melina, laughs: 'Like Sharon, I was really happy to be playing a strong female role. I think Melina was just the coolest thing. At one point I thought: "I defy anyone to come up with a situation she can't handle." That's what we girls were in there for. Sharon was out to get him and I was there to save him. Paul really knew how to play off the two of us in the movie.'

But Stone and Schwarzenegger were not always best of friends.

They are so similar, it is surprising they did not get on better. He is totally involved in his films. With *Total Recall* he was involved in the production and the marketing and, sitting in his hotel suite in Beverly Hills, said: 'I insisted on it. I want everybody on the film to feel they are part of the project. If they feel they are part of it they go all out for the movie. I want to be part of marketing. I know enough about it and the studios know I know enough about it.'

He got all he wanted, which included a $10 million fee and a hefty – never disclosed – percentage of the profits. But it is said that his shrewdly negotiated 'package' gave him a return on the film of more than $30 million.

At twenty, he was Mr Universe. At forty-two, in 1989, he was Mr Hollywood. He chews $8 cigars like the oldtime Hollywood moguls and his personal wealth is valued at more than $100 million. He owns several companies, has real estate interest in California and Colorado and is involved in several fitness/bodybuilding mail-order companies. In 1987, after an eight-year romance, he married the Kennedy Clan's Maria Shriver, but remained a staunch Republican, even commanding former President George Bush's fitness drive.

Arnold Schwarzenegger is an entrepreneurial American Dream lesson to anyone. To Sharon Stone, it was a Bible reading.

'We talked a lot on the set,' she says, adding: 'It seemed that our aims were so similar. We had come from humble places and wanted so much to make it in the movies. I learned from him that you *had* to sell yourself. We were not great soul buddies but I learned a lot.'

Schwarzenegger fills a room, not just by his bulk – 6ft 2ins tall; biceps: 22 ins; chest: 57ins; waist: 34 ins; thighs: 28 ins; calves: 20 ins – but also by his ambition always to be number one at what he does.

That is now Sharon Stone's creed. At 36B-24-36, she understood why Schwarzenegger had his own gym built on the set of *Total Recall*. He explained to her: 'I learned a long time ago in bodybuilding that if you want to have a great body you have to train four hours a day, have a special diet, sleep more, make certain sacrifices – there are no breaks. Three hundred pounds on a bench press will always feel like three hundred pounds . . . If you want something badly enough, you go through anything – no matter what it takes – and learn whatever you have to.'

A sickly child in Graz, Austria, he developed a Charles Atlas compulsion at fifteen years old. His hero was British bodybuilder and actor Reg Park, who used to appear in the Steve Reeves 1960s muscle and sandal film romps. He was twenty years old when he won the Mr Universe title in

London. He arrived in America in 1968 and fell in love with it. He had a problem with the language, but not with where he was going. He started a bricklaying business. 'I noticed that Americans loved things from other countries, so with my bodybuilding friend Franco Columbo, who was a trained bricklayer in Italy, we put advertisements in newspapers describing ourselves as "European bricklayers". Franco did the bricklaying and I was the guy, fancy dressed, who took the measurements and came up with the estimates.

'I bargained with the customers although all along I knew what the price would be. People in America like a deal. Americans feel more comfortable if they can make a deal – like in real estate, people bargain down from the asking price. I could sense there was some serious money in real estate so I saved every penny and started buying up small apartment buildings, office buildings, raw land . . . you have to learn to invest in yourself and also in what will pay off. As a professional athlete you learn about yourself, how you operate emotionally and mentally, what makes you turn on and be more aggressive and what makes you turn off. All of that helped me in the movies. More than anything, you learn discipline in sports, how to focus on one goal and go after it and leave other things aside.

'I'm not upset with my image, for it got me into the movies in the first place. It certainly wasn't my acting ability – that's for sure. But my goal is always to be the tops at the box-office.

'That's what I think everyone who works with me learns – that we're not making a movie that will bomb. We're making a WINNER.'

Which was why *Total Recall* was taking *Dick Tracy* and other movies that Sharon Stone had auditioned for out of the box-office running. During production, Schwarzenegger's wife Maria Shriver had flown down to Mexico City from Los Angeles to tell him that he was to be a father for the first time. And she met the co-stars, including Sharon Stone: 'When I met Sharon she was actually quite shy. She was very different from what people might think. She made an effort to get to know me, which I appreciated. There is a softness to Sharon that I think people are unaware of. They're intrigued by her image but don't know the person.'

She became an enormously different person between *Total Recall* and *Basic Instinct*, in that remarkable metamorphosis from want-to-be leading lady to celebrity-star. The time she spent in Mexico City and simply watching Schwarzenegger in control had completely changed her attitude.

She recalls with a smile the scene in *Total Recall* when Schwarzenegger finally kills her after a fantastic karate-kicking fight with the line: 'Consider that a divorce.'

'Arnold showed me this big bruise on his leg and he said: "I've been through all these action movies. I've done all this stuff in the jungles and look – *you* did this to me." I felt really big about that.'

She may have been killed in the movie, but in real life she believes all that training eventually saved her life.

She has a strange love-hate relationship with *Total Recall* and Schwarzenegger. Making the film was similar to her experiences with Steven Seagal – they were going for their goals, for the gold.

'I worked my ass off on *Total Recall* and someone said to me one day: "You know, Arnold doesn't like you." After thinking about that, I called this person in the hotel room and said: "Did anybody wonder if I liked Arnold? Or does only his opinion count because he's a star?"'

After *Total Recall*, *she* could kick some ass. But she couldn't compete with a Cadillac head-on on Sunset Boulevard. Her close encounter with death was the beginning of an altogether new Sharon Stone, emphasising the positive attitude she had learned on *Total Recall*. Meanwhile, Verhoeven was having to deal with another head-on collision. This one was between him and the critics.

Much was made of the one-liner 'Consider that a divorce', when Schwarzenegger blasts away 'wife' Sharon Stone. And the scene in which he picks up a man who has been mown down by machine-gun fire and uses him as a shield against more firepower, so that the corpse ends up with more holes than Bonnie and Clyde's car. Or the scene in which a body hurled on to the airless surface of Mars explodes, after internal pressure causes the eyeballs to pop out. There are countless crunchy-sounding back- and neck-breakings, facial stabbings and decapitation. One critic said that if someone is killed by plain old gunfire in a Verhoeven movie they are lucky indeed. But the Motion Picture Association of America (MPAA) is concerned with overall impact rather than individual scenes.

Many times the MPAA has said that it does not pass artistic judgment but issue ratings – Parental Guidance, Restricted and the box-office killer, an X – to keep children from being exposed to things their parents do not wish them to see. *Total Recall* got an R – restricted to children aged under seventeen years old, unless accompanied by an adult, and was off and running at the box-office. Critics of the system point out that smaller, independently produced and distributed films like Pedro Almodovar's *Tie Me Up! Tie Me Down!* received an X-rating, yet contained nothing more graphic than several R films. The MPAA defends itself by saying there is good and bad sex in film and it is a question of balance. But they do not make artistic judgments.

The fine-line issue would later put at risk the mainstream distribution of *Basic Instinct* and, by that threat, hundreds of millions of dollars.

Unlike other directors, Verhoeven believes he can have the best of both worlds, artistic freedom and mainstream rating: 'With *Total Recall* they were very nice. They said it was a pleasure to watch, but too strong for an R.

'Could I tone it down? It was very different than with *Robocop*, when we had to go back seven or eight times to get an R. I conferred with Arnold and the writers and we took certain things completely out – such as some of the girl parts, when a dwarf hooker slices a bad guy's belly. I think the editing improved the film. Whereas on *Robocop*, it changed the feel – it had much more of a comic-book touch, originally, much more over the top. The cuts took that away.'

There were two key issues which Verhoeven would have to face up to again in the Hollywood of the 1990s – censorship and political correctness. In 1990, the MPAA had brought in NC-17 rating, a non-pornographic rating allowing no one under seventeen to attend screenings. For major studios, an NC-17 was a profit killer.

Nevertheless, Verhoeven says he would rather deal with the MPAA than the film authorities back in Holland: 'Since films there are government-subsidised, the scripts are subject to pre-production censorship. I prefer to deal with it this way, with small adjustments.' Of the violence inherent in his work, he says it goes back to his days in The Hague during the German occupation, memories of fires, bombs and destruction. He says his teenage daughters have no delusions about violence. They see it in their day-to-day life: 'The reality in the streets and in schools is much worse than what's in the movies. Kids don't have to be protected. I would let my daughters see my films when they were younger but I would explain how the effects are done. Kids of eight or nine could see *Total Recall*.

'Movies reflect society and society is the problem. That is where you have to solve it. Movies are easy scapegoats.'

Just like easy talk around hot Hollywood blondes. And the world's sexual mores.

10

All is Revealed

'I heard that Kathleen Turner's husband told her: "I may not be the best lover in the world but I know what you like." That's being the best lover in the world.'

– Sharon Stone, 1990

Sharon Stone believes it was only her fitness and strength, developed during the training for *Total Recall*, that allowed her to live after her car crash.

'I was driving home from acting class. It was the sleaziest part of Sunset Boulevard with a strip joint across the street and the cops picking up the hookers to take them behind the building . . . A woman who turned out to be an illegal immigrant was driving on the wrong side of the street. I wrote off my BMW. I was so in shock that most of the time I didn't know I was hurt. I sat on the street for three hours. Nobody recognised me. I had a broken rib, dislocated jaw, sprained back and twisted knee.

'I was a crying, hysterical woman with a crashed car, sitting on a street corner, staring into space. I woke up the next morning and tried to get out of bed and walked halfway through the house and then just lay down on the floor and cried.

'I had concussion and didn't know the shape I was in. Once I got examined it was such a mess. I had months and months of physical therapy in recovery – a back brace and a clavicle collar. Even after the hospital I had to stay at home with the surgical brace and collar. But it was time to find out who my real friends were. Some of them who I thought would be wonderful did not want to know once I was off the scene. I realised I was one of those "life-of-the-party" girls. Once I was in bed with a broken body and could not be entertaining they were not around anymore. So these friends were given a big clear-out. But the advantage was that the friends I did not expect anything from were around to help.

'The doctor told me I probably wouldn't have walked again if I hadn't been in such good shape. Even though I haven't tried to keep up the level of routine I did during *Total Recall*, I feel the quality of my life was improved by it – saved by it really. And I owe that to Arnold. I learned from him that you get nothing for nothing. You have to work your ass off. And that's why you get success.'

The accident provoked Sharon Stone into much thought. Physically she was trapped by her clavicle collar and back brace and she had to learn how to use her body again, to make it work. 'I'm into a different kind of fitness now,' she said in 1994. 'I don't want big muscles now, but at the time it saved my life.'

It was a retrospective period: 'I spent months afterwards sitting alone in my house. That's when I decided things had to change or I was never going to work again. Realising I might have been killed and having a lot of time to sit around and think made me wonder. I was tired of it all. I didn't know what was going to happen next.

'I was asked to give the Commencement Speech at my high school that year and when I thought things out to write them down I realised that I had to make changes.

'One of the things was this: when you are in high school your success is measured by how much you are like everybody else. But from the second you graduate, and on to the end of your life, it's measured by how much of an individual you are. It made me realise that it was time to stop accepting things other than what was truly me.

'The *Total Recall* experience did everything for me. It gave me box-office viability. Everybody knew who I was then. Not that I was Sharon Stone – I was the girl in that hit movie. I *was* the girl in *Total Recall*.

'It made so much sense to move on as positively as I could from there. Anything else would just have been wasting chances.

'It was a physical role and I think they were looking for someone tall and athletic – really extroverted. You know, when she rolls across to Arnold who has been complaining about bad dreams, undoes the top of her mini-nightgown and purrs: "I'll give you something to dream about."

'That's me. I studied karate for the film and got pretty well bruised – on my jaw. I'd walk into a party and they'd think my boyfriend beat me up. It was the first time I got that vibe about what battered women go through.'

But what about non-abused women, what about ageism in Hollywood? 'Oh, I don't give a damn about age. I've thought of actresses trying to resist who they are, to be younger. They do this, they do that – it's just ridiculous. Ultimately the greatest gift you can give is your individuality. I don't think there's anything wrong with a woman being in her thirties. I earned every single one of my years. Unfortunately, society has deemed that when women reach forty they lose their sex appeal. I have every intention on going on TV when I'm forty (in 1999 – remember) and saying: "Hey, I'm forty. No sex appeal? Ha, ha, ha."'

She says it was a tilt against the ageism attitude as well as a desperate career move which convinced her to pose for *Playboy*. 'They had been after me for a long time, but I couldn't bring myself to do it. I had this kind of voice when I was a young teenager, a woman's body when I was a younger girl, a sophisticated intellect but a very naïve character. That made it difficult for me to do what I had to do. Later, when I felt right about it, I did it. Besides, I'd met ten Playmates and I hadn't met one with a PERFECT body, and that changed my attitude. I thought: "They look pretty good in the pictures. We're all human."' Some more than others.

'She's smart,' says Barry Diller, who is the boss of the 1990s television future, the home shopping network QVC, but who earned his showbusiness medals as the chairman of both Paramount and 20th Century Fox Studios. Diller, a legend in deal- and star-making, instantly recognised Stone as a winner: 'She's sharp, which is more than you can say for most people who get photographed with some of their clothes off.'

Which Sharon Stone did rather spectacularly in *Playboy* of July 1990 (no back copies available). She is pictured in scenes from *Total Recall*. In one, as Schwarzenegger's wife Lori, she is seen in bed with the muscle man and, in another, pointing a gun at him. Then there are more explicit pictures by Phillip Dixon, including the cover-shot with the headline: 'She's Got Hollywood Breathing Heavy.'

Intentionally.

The 1990 photo layout is in black-and-white. Sharon Stone knows ageism exists – everywhere. 'You don't photograph thirty-two-year-old things in colour. No, no, NO!'

It didn't make the pictures less exotic.

'She was very adventurous,' recalls Dixon, adding: 'She suggested more risqué things than I wanted to do. She scaled a narrow fire escape ladder wearing only spiked heels and panties! She went all the way up, all forty feet to the top of the ladder. She was prepared to do anything to make the picture session a success. She was the complete professional.'

But in the text that accompanied the pictures, which included one of her splayed across an unmade bed, she was not altogether diplomatic as she talked about Los Angeles: 'People here are more concerned with being fashionable than being decent.'

She maintains she didn't wear any make-up for the *Playboy* pictures, but Johnny Herandez of Cloutier – the make-up company who work with Madonna and most of the Hollywood crowd – is credited in the magazine for 'hair and make-up'. Certainly, there was not a lot of cover-up. In one picture she is on full display. 'The photographer wanted me as I am and that was just fine. Wet hair, no make-up, no clothes. That's just as naked as you can get. A director once said to me: "The reason men want you to wear make-up is that, when you don't, they feel they have to be honest with you because you're honest with them."'

Stone said the obligatory things in her remarks to complement the remarkable photographs of herself: 'I heard that Kathleen Turner's husband told her: "I may not be the best lover in the world but I know what you like." That's being the best lover in the world.

'Masculine men are an endangered species. *We've endangered* them by not experiencing our equality as women, but trying to be like men. It's an enormous mistake. And we're afraid that if we reveal ourselves sexually to a person he will steal our soul. So we pick people who could never possibly do that – people who are bad for us.'

Playboy was good for her. By 1994, she said she was bored, talking about the stapled spread – but she would, wouldn't she? – but she answers the question of what made her do it. 'One, I wanted to be seen. Leading ladies my age are typed and you need to be sexually appealing for parts in the movies you might be right for. It's a man's world and when you look like I look, that's what it is. I'd taken my top off in three movies and nobody noticed. I felt I was re-owning my femininity.

'I don't want to be a man. And it's not an option that I'll ever be Meryl Streep. Also, to be absolutely frank, it was like four or five days after wrapping *Total Recall* and I'd put every dime I had into buying a house. I really needed some work.'

'Sharon looked absolutely amazing in the pictures,' says Paul Verhoeven, adding: 'Between her and Arnold, they sold the picture. Of course, they had their personal interests at heart, but don't we all? If the project succeeds we all succeed. It's too much of a gamble, too much money is involved today to be concerned with one part of the work. We all have to go for it together.'

Verhoeven was to be Sharon Stone's saviour. And, as it turned out, she played the same role for him. They were the two who helped make *Basic Instinct* one of the cinema's great financial successes and changed the rules of mainstream film-making for ever more. Along with Michael Douglas – it was again a meeting of minds as well as well-toned bodies – Stone scorched up the screen. Douglas, a second generation Hollywood icon, has never acknowledged any disparity with making high- or low-brow movies, as long as they make money. Everyone involved in *Basic Instinct* made history.

It wasn't easy. You have to wonder if there were devilish forces – as Paul Verhoeven would call them – at work.

After the film was completed, Verhoeven got involved in pre-production talks to do a high-profile pirate movie with Geena Davis as the sexy pirate-in-chief. It never could seem to work out. Sharon Stone was persuaded to star in the voyeuristic thriller *Sliver* which, although it didn't make her Hollywood career, it didn't hurt in Tinseltown or overseas. But she felt her new star status had been exploited.

Also after the film was completed, Michael Douglas was caught in suite 719 at the Regent Beverly Wiltshire Hotel in Beverly Hills with his wife's best friend. Tragically, it was Douglas' wife Diandra who walked in on the couple, and many lurid tabloid headlines followed.

He then spent thirty days at $19,500 a day at a sex addiction clinic. In 1987, Michael Douglas played a happily married lawyer who has a weekend sexual fling with a woman who emerges as a psychotic sociopath, Richard the Second in stiletto heels. The 1980s message was the dangers of one-night stands and extra-marital affairs. In the movie, Douglas and his family were terrorised as a result of his lust, even the pet bunny rabbit got boiled by Glenn Close's evil Alex Forrest.

Five years later, the message of *Basic Instinct* was that any sort of sex can be dangerous to your health. Full stop.

It was the theme of the script by Joe Eszterhas. And he can be a dangerous and difficult man . . . a madman or a movie messiah, depending on where you are standing.

11

A True Hollywood Tale

'. . . and Fuck You'
Screenwriter Joe Eszterhas in an 1989 letter to
Michael Ovitz, regarded as the most powerful man
in Hollywood

Sharon Stone was to remain a major force and power in
Hollywood because of what she learned during the making of
Basic Instinct, a film which involved one of the most extra-
ordinary creative power struggles in the first century of
making movies. The ingredients were volatile. Michael
Douglas is one of the half-dozen most successful leading men
in the world, Paul Verhoeven one of a handful of top box-office
directors, and Joe Eszterhas, the mega-hot writer of the 1990s.
And all three of them are used to getting their own way.

Eszterhas' *Basic Instinct* script was bought at auction in the
summer of 1990 by Carolco Pictures for a price that, even in
pre-recession days' easy-money Hollywood, sent the town
into an orgy of gossip buzz. They paid $3 million for the 120-
page story involving an ice-pick serial murderer on the prowl
in San Francisco. She's baffling, brilliant and omnivorously
omnisexual.

Michael Douglas is the troubled police detective on the
trail. He investigates the murder of a one-time high-profile
rock star. The evidence includes a blood-soaked ice pick, a
woman's flimsy white scarf tied to a bedpost and the remains
of a torrid sexual encounter. Douglas, Nick Curran, is drawn
into the web by Catherine Tramell, who writes books about

'fictional' murders, uses ice picks to make lumps of ice to cool her vodka and tonics and has a penchant for female lovers as well as men.

Eszterhas' script often gets straight to the point. Detective Nick's partner, seeing he is falling for the possibly dangerous charms of Catherine Tramell, shoots him a smile and the line: 'Well, she's got that magna cum laude pussy on her that done fried up your brain.' Then there's Douglas' line (as Curran), when he finds out that his suspect and another woman, her friend, Roxy, are lovers: 'Tell me Roxy, man to man. I think she's the fuck of the century, don't you?'

Well, actually, in Hollywood terms, that was in Joe Eszterhas' letter to Michael Ovitz, the head of Creative Artists Agency, which represents deal-makers and talent around the world. The Eszterhas' attitude didn't surprise those who knew him well.

'Joe is a strong person. He's had to fight for everything he got,' says Michael Roberts, editor of *Boston* magazine, who used to work with Eszterhas in the late 1960s at the *Cleveland Plain Dealer* in Ohio. Eszterhas, who was fifty in 1994, was born in Hungary during the upheaval of World War Two. His mother was a schizophrenic and his father a novelist. Roberts says: "That's what forged this guy. He's got cast-iron balls. Once he gets going on crusades he's a damn hard man to deal with. He gets those squinty eyes and that shitty look and you say: "Oh, no, no, not again."' In Ohio they made fun of the teenage immigrant kid with the strange accent and he started breaking heads. At fourteen, he nearly killed another teenager with a baseball bat and then decided to put all his anger and energy into reading; he had seen his own dark side. Hundreds of novels and college later, he became a general reporter on the *Cleveland Plain Dealer* and then moved to San Francisco, to become a major writer for the growingly influential *Rolling Stone* magazine. He then began screenwriting.

One of his first scripts was *F.I.S.T.*, a union drama with shades of Brando in *On The Waterfront* in 1954. It sold for

$80,000 and interested Sylvester Stallone. Stallone started to rewrite the screenplay. Eszterhas immediately called him an 'egomaniac' and admitted: 'I went crazy. I said this was mine, he was trying to steal my script. I was Rocky Balboa and he was Apollo Creed. I said: "I've been in more bar-room fights than Sly – he fights like a sissy."'

Workers on *F.I.S.T.* say the writer and Stallone were a perfect match. They enjoyed the conflict and, a year later, made up. 'Joe's morality is what's good for Joe,' said one Hollywood worker. Another called him simply 'a bully'.

He certainly is a big bulk of a man, with a bushy beard and, yes, at times, these shitty looking eyes. They were evident in his dealings with former Columbia Studios boss Frank Price. Columbia were buying his *Jagged Edge* for half a million dollars and the studio boss wanted a more conventional ending. In turn, Eszterhas made changes, but the final conclusion to the Glenn Close, Jeff Bridges, Robert Loggia film stayed ambivalent.

'It depends who is asking him for changes,' said a colleague. 'After Joe had won his fight with Frank Price and got his half a million bucks, he incorporated many changes suggested by others. It depends who is saying it to him and why and in what tone. If he feels someone is coming down on him for the sake of coming down on him, then he steels his backbone and goes crazy.'

He went crazy on *Basic Instinct*, but there were storms starting and fading and then whirling up again around the whole project. From the moment Carolco had bought Eszterhas' *Basic Instinct* script, there was never an easy day. He maintains it isn't an easy life. In 1989, the writer responsible for *Betrayed* (with Debra Winger) and *Music Box* (with Jessica Lange) left Creative Artists Agency, accusing Michael Ovitz of threatening to blackball him. 'I simply can't function on a day to day basis with you . . . without feeling myself dirtied. So do what you must do, Mike, and fuck you.'

The letter went public in the Hollywood trade papers, then

the *Los Angeles Times* and *The New York Times* and then around
the dining-table times of Hollywood's information factories.
Eszterhas' career was as good as dead.

Ovitz had every reason to be upset. Eszterhas' scripts were
then selling for around $1.25 million each. The super-agent,
who remained the number one man in Hollywood, was
alleged to have said or written to Eszterhas: 'My foot soldiers
who go up and down Wilshire Boulevard [in Beverly Hills]
each day will blow your brains out.' One read that *not* literally,
but that Ovitz's talent agents would block all deals with
Eszterhas, who countered that he had sold his new $1.2 mil-
lion home because of Ovitz's 'threats and the uncertainty they
cast on my future.'

Eszterhas went back to his former agent, Guy McElwaine –
Sharon Stone's agent in 1994 – who himself had just returned
to International Creative Management (ICM), Ovitz's main
rival in terms of the status of their stable of clients.

Nine months later, Eszterhas sold the *Basic Instinct* script
and, lavishly paid, wandered into the biggest storm of his
career. That far.

The Hemingway-lookalike writer, who favours open-
necked Hawaiian shirts, was executive producer on the film
and Irwin Winkler, who previously had produced the
Eszterhas-written films *Betrayed* and *Music Box*, was being
paid $1 million to produce *Basic Instinct*. The duo walked off
the film three weeks after selling the script to Carolco.

They objected, they said, to Paul Verhoeven's plans to add
lesbian love scenes and spice up the already breakthrough
and sizzling sex scenes.

Verhoeven recalls: 'It was a big revelation when I first
went to America to find that sexuality was so pushed under
the table. When I read this script I felt compelled – like a
naughty child, basically – to say: "Listen, guys. This is what
is happening, isn't it? So why worry about it? I'll just shoot
it."'

That was a little too provocative for the 'sensitive'

Eszterhas. Verhoeven was paid $5 million to direct, Michael Douglas, $15 million to star and Sharon Stone $250,000 to get naked and horizontal with him. The first story conference did not go well. Verhoeven reports: 'When I first read the script I was wrong. I read it really superficially. I felt that because it involved a lot of heterosexual sex and some lesbian characters, some homosexual sex would be necessary to balance that. I expressed my opinion of that to Joe – not in the nicest way, probably – and Joe got upset. He and Winkler walked out.'

The writer and producer said they were offended by Verhoeven's plans to make the psychological thriller even more sexually explicit. Winkler remembers: 'Verhoeven had no idea what the script was about. And he seemed to be solely interested in how much nudity he could get from the actors . . . how much skin they could show. Verhoeven wanted to show body parts in various stages of excitement.'

Eszterhas claims Verhoeven told him: 'I am the director, *ja*? I am right and you are wrong.' The writer says he was amazed: 'This movie is already a very erotic mystery. The focus has to go on subtlety and on acting. If you hype the sex, the whole apple-cart gets upset. You get dang close to walking across the porn-line. It sensationalises the material. He seemed solely interested in emphasising and sensationalising the erotic aspects of my script.'

But, of course, the material was already sensational. And erotic. The 'hot sexy thriller' Michael Douglas wanted to make. Douglas had never indicated that he wanted to make statements: 'I wanted to do it for the sexuality, for the fact of just doing a sexy-type picture.'

Carolco stood by Verhoeven and Michael Douglas and turned down a request by the producer and writer to buy back the script. They then allowed the two men to leave the film, but keep their combined total of $4 million in fees.

Verhoeven spent six months with *Total Recall* writer Gary Goldman, trying to put some gay sex into the movie without being offensive to the mainstream audience or to gays. Then, he believed Eszterhas was right. 'Dramatically, a lesbian scene didn't make any sense because the script was not about that, really. It would just be gratuitous. At the outset, I did not see the basement of this building. Later, I discovered this basement, the heart of the script. It would be foolish to build the wrong building on top of that. Our second draft was the furthest from the Eszterhas screenplay; by the fifth draft we were moving back to Joe's original words.'

In the spring of 1991, everyone involved had a surprising reconciliation. Carolco had sent Eszterhas a copy of the revised *Basic Instinct* script on 7 March 1991, and by 1 April that year, they seemed to be best friends. Eszterhas explained about receiving the revised script: 'I was flabbergasted. There were maybe half a dozen, a dozen line changes – no plot point, no character changes – there were just some visual changes that Paul had brought in.'

The nasty public feud was over. Verhoeven had admitted a mistake, something rare in such a major player.

But not everyone was happy about the reconciliation. Rich Jennings, who in 1992 was executive director of the Gay and Lesbian Alliance (GLAAD) in Los Angeles, had heard about and read Eszterhas' *Basic Instinct* script in the summer of 1990. Later, he had called Verhoeven and was told that Eszterhas and Winkler – who was replaced by producer Alan Marshall – were no longer involved. The director told Jennings that much rewriting had been done and the GLAAD leader says he was relieved to find Verhoeven 'so sympathetic'.

Then it all changed. Hollywood reconciliation, like the more complex resurrection, is always possible if the stakes are high enough. Eszterhas was gushingly and publicly polite about Verhoeven and the director's lack of ego. He also insisted his screenplay was not homophobic – he was a man who wrote about persecution of minorities, of the odd-men-and-women out.

San Francisco Supervisor Harvey Milk is one of the most

high-profile gay politicians in America. His aide, Rick Ruvolo, reacted for him in the first place about the *Basic Instinct* script: 'It's a disgusting story. It's trash.'

Summer was early on the streets of San Francisco in 1991 and the evenings were warm. The temperature would remain constant, but the atmosphere around the filming on *Basic Instinct* was much hotter. Inside the Tosca Café one evening, they were filming a scene. The arc lights were blazing and the sound booms in position. The technicians were quietly gathered around the urns of iced tea and tepid coffee as a disembodied voice barked: 'Action.' Michael Douglas was a figure in black from his jeans to his sunglasses to his shiny slicked-back hair as he moved on his cue.

'Michael Douglas – Fuck You! Michael Douglas – Racist, Sexist, Anti-Gay!' The protesters on the streets chanted and waved placards reading: 'Stop Hate!' and 'Hollywood Greed Kills'. Militants paint-bombed the film set. Often, Douglas and Stone had to be discreetly guarded as they left locations and climbed into waiting cars.

Stone says she had never experienced problems with the gay community: 'I was a model before I worked as an actress and the gay community is an active part of the fashion business. Many of my dating experiences included me and my date and a gay couple. So I was sensitive to issues that would concern gay people. That's why the flap over *Basic Instinct* was beyond my comprehension. My perspective of the lesbian relationship in the film was that it was a pure, loving relationship. At the same time Catherine was clearly not a lesbian – she was a party girl.

'This was a unique opportunity for the gay community to use a big media event as a way to be heard. That was good. I'm enormously sympathetic with the issue that was raised. I'm enormously sympathetic because I know that the focus is always on the blonde people in the movies.

'Where are the interracial relationships? Where are the Puerto Rican men and women? If there weren't incredible racial issues, Billy Dee Williams would have been one of our biggest movie stars – a fine, talented, gorgeous, charismatic actor. Why is that? It's not right. It's not fair.

'I'm sympathetic in terms of all minority groups. I believe that even though women are not a minority we are treated like one. So many female characters are written the way men experience women or would like to experience women. But that's not the way women really are. How often do you go to a movie and see a female character who's like a woman you actually know? I think *Basic Instinct* showed both men and women in the trenches pitted against one another.'

Such words did not appease the protesters. 'The characters embody all the negative stereotypes about lesbians,' argued GLAAD's Richard Jennings. Groups also objected to a 'date-rape' scene between Douglas and Jeanne Tripplehorn, making her screen debut aged 28 in 1992.

The film became about creative control, minority-group pressure and politics as much as about the characters, good and bad, off screen and on. And about sex for sensation – is it to sell tickets or tell the story? GLAAD sent letters to American film critics, claiming 'no major Hollywood studio has ever produced a film with a lesbian protagonist with positive and redeeming qualities.' They said they were going to disrupt the 1992 Oscars in protest, but didn't make enough of an impact. Ironically, a year later Sharon Stone was the star of the 1993 Oscars, one of the glamour queens of the evening.

But that evening outside the Tosca Café, the disharmony around the production continued. Even after a court order had been issued prohibiting excessive noise and the use of flashlights, and temporary restraining orders for the activists to stay one hundred feet away from the film-makers, the protests, by GLAAD and other groups, like Queer Nation, continued. There were more than a dozen arrests.

'This has been a strange shoot,' said Michael Douglas, with wry understatement, adding: 'It's been strange from the beginning.'

Carolco had a huge investment in the film and there was a plus to the protests. The film would become a 'must-see' movie – how else could people judge for themselves? Although the majority of protesters knew little of the film, they were making judgments.

Douglas' detective is straight, in the sexual sense, but far removed from the gawky nice Police Inspector Keller he played for five years on television's *The Streets of San Francisco*. The gay groups despised what they knew of the film, which was that lesbian or bisexual women killed straight men. They wanted the characters of the female villains 'softened'. They wanted Douglas' cop to be played by a woman, charging the movie was 'clearly homophobic, lesbophobic, a film which once again inverts the realities of our lives'. A fund-raising lunch for AIDS organisations on the set of *Basic Instinct* and hosted by Michael Douglas did not quell the controversy. But it did precede the astonishing sub-plot.

All involved agreed something had to be done. The film-makers, Verhoeven, Michael Douglas, Eszterhas, and producer Alan Marshall agreed to a meeting with gay group leaders. It all smacked of 'politically correct' censorship. Executives at Carolco and Tri-Star Pictures (which comes under the Japanese Sony umbrella), who would distribute the film worldwide, insisted on a strong hand in dealing with what could be a Hollywood nightmare – the vetting of enter-tainment by special interest groups. 'Censorship by street action would not be tolerated,' was the official word from the executive suites of Hollywood.

Douglas, Verhoeven and Alan Marshall agreed. But at the meeting Eszterhas disagreed. 'Suddenly – in fact, to my big amazement – Joe told the protesters: "OK, you're right. The script is insensitive and I don't want to hurt you and I'm going to change it,"' reported Verhoeven.

The director and Michael Douglas believe that Eszterhas betrayed them while they were in full production. 'I was most offended by Joe's actions,' is all Douglas will quietly say about what happened. As far as the protests and his return to San Francisco were concerned, he sighed and shrugged his shoulders and said: 'The San Francisco return wasn't a lot of fun, given the gay/lesbian demonstrations that were going on. It was very disappointing and I was surprised at a town that is as liberal as San Francisco is, that prides itself on accepting people of all backgrounds, which is one of the reasons why there's such a strong gay/lesbian population there, not to be more open and understanding about our rights in letting us shoot the film.'

Verhoeven says of the changes Eszterhas made in the script: 'I felt they were not changes made for the sake of the script. They were changes for the sake of pleasing the gay community. I felt they were dramatically incorrect and weakened the characters. All of them were inspired, not by the desire to make a better movie, but to market a movie in which all the characters would always be politically correct. I have the highest respect for Joe's writing and I think this is one of his best scripts. It was nearly perfect from the beginning and it still is. I think that basically, in his heart, Joe knows that's true.'

The rewrites were rejected, not because they would have cost $3 million in re-filming, but 'because they would have undermined the strength of Eszterhas' original material and weakened the characters which he had so vividly portrayed and lessened the integrity of the picture itself'. Unofficially, Carolco was calling the changes 'patronising drivel'.

Police in riot gear had to be called to locations after word of the decision spread around the San Francisco gay community. Alan Marshall made twenty-five citizen's arrests.

Critics of Eszterhas say he had no power to make changes in the film and simply wanted to be a hero to the gay and lesbian communities. He says that's nonsense and that scripts are changed in production all the time. 'I don't enjoy pissing people off. What was I supposed to do? Walk out of that room saying these gay people are full of shit? I'm not going to change anything. I would have been lying to myself and lying to them. I've written three movies specifically about intolerance and injustice done to a minority group. I don't want to be part of anything that lends itself to gay-bashing. But minority groups have got to accept the possibility that among them is a sociopath. Is it wise that the only villains we ever see on the screen are WASPs?'

Verhoeven regards it differently. He said of the gay groups: 'They read the script like fundamentalists read the Bible. They could not visualise the film. All the protests were based on people having read the script and we all know that reading a script is a difficult thing, and I have misread several scripts in my life. I threw the script of *Robocop* out of the window nearly, because I thought it was so bad, and my wife picked it up and read it and said I should read it again. I am a professional – I am supposed to be able to read scripts. It's difficult. It's just a blueprint of a house that's not there, and I think what happened is that they picked on certain lines and didn't realise they were lines said by characters that had certain flaws. Characters should not be correct for drama because then there is no drama. That's what a drama is about, and they took lines out of context, put them together, and said that's what we were doing. I think something like that is what happened. They wanted every character in the film to be politically correct. I mean if you have all OK characters you have no drama left – it's like Paradise on earth.'

But Tammy Bruce, who was President of the National Organisation of Women's Los Angeles branch in 1992, argued that Jodie Foster's FBI rookie in *Silence of the Lambs*, the controversial film which won Sir Anthony Hopkins an Oscar for his portrayal of serial killer Hannibal 'The Cannibal' Lecter, was a better role-model: 'There's a big difference between a powerful woman's role like that one and a misogynist like this. Lesbianism is used as titillation of men and to provoke men in the film. It's also used as a shorthand for evil and for all sorts of pathology.'

Sharon Stone's reaction to that was: 'My character is socio-pathic and motivated by power – gender choice is a secondary and irrelevant issue for her.'

Verhoeven argues: 'Sex was never the standpoint of the movie. I always thought the movie was about evil.'

With lots of sexy characters.

After all the outcry by gay and lesbian groups when *Basic Instinct* was released in cinemas, Sharon Stone discovered she had a lesbian following. Even a fan club. She was asked how that felt. 'Mmmm, it makes me feel good.'

The film was going to earn her more than a fan club. Her whole world was going to be rocked.

She was going to owe a lot of it to Michael Douglas and her own inherent bravado. Douglas claims that she had 'more balls' than anyone else on the film set. He helped make Kathleen Turner a superstar in *Romancing the Stone* in 1984, and allowed Glenn Close to steal all the gleeful mayhem she could from *Fatal Attraction* in 1987.

Once again, he was going to help establish a worldwide star in a twisted love story about homicidal impulse and thrill killing.

Are you sitting comfortably?

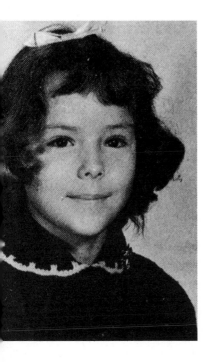

The dark roots of things to come. Sharon as a youngster
(All Action)

Basic swimsuit! (All Action)

From frock to France!
(Above: All Action.
Right: Popperfoto)

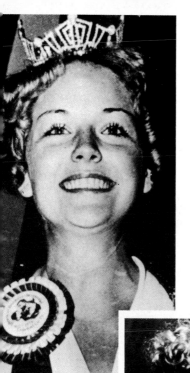

**From Miss Crawford County to
Miss Confidence**
(Left: All Action.
Below: Frank Spooner Pictures)

Family girl. Sharon with her father **John** (London Features), **her sister Alison** (London Features), **her teddy bear** (Frank Spooner Pictures) **and her first husband Michael Greenburgh** (London Features)

(Top left) **Sharon Stone with
Richard Chamberlain in *King
Solomon's Mines*** (Kobal Collection),
(above right) **with Dylan McDermot in
*Where Sleeping Dogs Lie*** (Alpha) **and**
(above left) **with Christopher Rydell in
*Blood and Sand***
(Moviestore Collection)

More men in her life!
(Above left) **Stone with Dwight Yoakam** (London Features), (above right) **with George Burns** (Reuters/Bettmann), (above) **with Valentino** (John Van Hasselt, Sygma) **and** (below right) **with George Michael** (London Features)

**The big man in her life - Sharon with Arnold
Schwarzenegger in *Total Recall*** (Alpha)

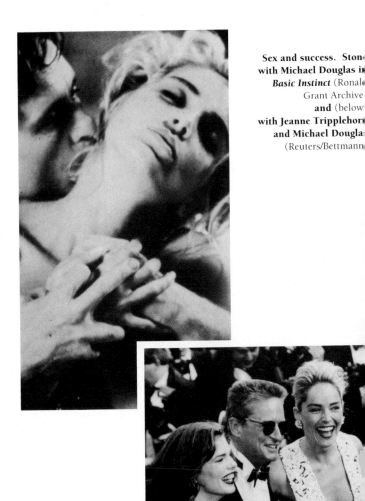

Sex and success. Stone
with Michael Douglas in
Basic Instinct (Ronald
Grant Archive)
and (below)
with Jeanne Tripplehorn
and Michael Douglas
(Reuters/Bettmann)

The Flash (Kobal Collection)

With *Basic Instinct* director Paul Verhoeven (Reuters/Bettmann)

(Alpha)

(Famous)

(London Features)

(Frank Spooner Pictures)

She's everywhere!

Maybe one day!
(London Features)

**Sharon Stone announcing Oscar
nominees in March 1993**
(Reuters/Bettmann)

Love and Hate - the two Bills. (Above) **With Billy Baldwin in** *Sliver* **and** (right) **with Bill MacDonald to whom she was engaged in 1993** (Alpha)

(Right) **Sharon with Bob Wagner**
(All Action) **and** (below) **with
Sylvester Stallone in
*The Specialist*** (Alpha)

(All Action)

(Sygma)

(Sygma)

(Sygma)

Stone in *The Quick and the Dead*

The Blonde Bombshell (Moviestore Collection)

12

Kiss Kiss

'Can you lick her nipple a bit more?'
Paul Verhoeven on directing
Sharon Stone and Michael Douglas
in *Basic Instinct*, 1991

The trouble on the streets of San Francisco and in the executive suites in Hollywood off-screen and the red-hot material they were trying to portray on screen conjured up a tight mix of tension and paranoia. There was even greater pressure on Sharon Stone. With all the publicity and outcry, she and the movie *had* to deliver.

She had the help of Michael Douglas who, like Clint Eastwood, runs one of the most admired film production companies in Hollywood. Douglas was not involved officially as a producer of *Basic Instinct*, but he helped Verhoeven and other executives on the film set an extremely high professional tone. This wasn't a giggle, some naughty nudie. This was business. And Michael Douglas has always been an excellent businessman.

Joe Eszterhas had suggested a disclaimer that might run at the start of *Basic Instinct* along the lines of 'This is fiction . . .' Controlling a sneer, Michael Douglas shot back: 'A disclaimer? Sure, we'll run that. Why didn't we have a disclaimer before *Wall Street* that said: "This doesn't mean that every Wall Street banker is a crook. Or before *Fatal Attraction* – this doesn't mean every single woman is a psycho . . ."' He irritates easily.

Sharon Stone found that out quickly. Michael Douglas had to be persuaded to go to bed with her at work. It was hard work – at first.

Douglas, who had played a twentysomething in a flashback scene in *The War of the Roses* – 'diet and fucking, fucking facials,' he complained to me at the Four Seasons Hotel in Beverly Hill – was in perfect shape to let it all, literally, hang out with Sharon Stone.

Of course, she already believed this was her best and possibly her last shot at major acclaim and fame. She had nothing to hide.

The *Basic Instinct* sex scenes went all the way, and she laughed and asked: 'Do you have sex like that? Do you know women who have orgasms from these anatomically impossible positions? In two minutes? Please. Send them over to my house so I can learn.

'Once I realised that was what the guys wanted, I thought: "Oh, I get it. No matter how he touches her or where he touches her or what else he does to her, it's the most, it's the best, it's the sexiest." That's the Fuck of the Century according to the macho-man mentality. Women want men to see them and experience them and take time with them.

'I don't think women want to be slammed up against the wall and tied to the sofa. But "the fuck of the century" became a fantasy for women too. They thought: "He can do that. I hear he got $14 million to do that! I'd give you $14 million if you could do that to me, buddy!"'

Which is what someone blonde and busty is doing to the rakish Mick Jagger-style rock star in the opening scene of *Basic Instinct*. Verhoeven obviously intended to hide the identity of the wildly abandoned seductress, but admitted: 'Sharon did all of that. I think a lot of people are still discussing the size of her breasts in comparison with the other scenes. Sharon did that opening scene and was splendid.'

'I don't do what I do for the money,' says Sharon Stone on a warm spring day in West Hollywood. 'I do what I do for a different kind of gratification, and the opportunity to explore things that I haven't explored before in other characters. That's what's thrilling to me. Of course, it's scary to look at these parts of yourself that you want to pretend don't exist.

'And the more I had to commit to doing that, the scarier it got, but when you are playing a part like that you can't look at it and judge it. You have to look at it and own it, and I found that by the time I was done with the movie I wasn't as bad as I thought I was before I started.'

Verhoeven says: 'Sharon was brilliant and powerful and in complete control – not a victim.'

Michael Douglas says of the film: 'While *Fatal Attraction* was a picture close to home for a lot of people, because you could identify with these characters, it was a reality tale, while *Basic Instinct* is like a detective novel people like to read in the privacy of their own homes. It's almost Gothic. It was certainly more dramatic. The real question here is – is anybody really worth redemption?'

Finally, he thought he was. The son of Kirk Douglas, the former Issur Danielovitch, and his British wife Diana Dill, he won the Best Actor Oscar for playing sartorial sinner Gordon Gekko in director Oliver Stone's *Wall Street* and then ran back-to-back in films with *Black Rain* and *The War of the Roses*.

When he finally agreed to Sharon Stone as his co-star in *Basic Instinct*, he was a confident man. 'I don't have to prove anything to myself, to the industry, to my father. I've become at peace with myself on a lot of different levels and areas. I'd just like to improve my golf game and play some tennis.'

But his piercing green eyes deny that remark. More importantly, in 1994, with grey power on manoeuvres around his hairline, he was anxious to prove he is still a sexual star. Which is what he believes he is in the business for. As a producer-actor on projects like *Romancing the Stone* and *Jewel of the Nile*, and producer of the Oscar cavalcade *One Flew Over the Cuckoo's Nest*, he has always had to cope with movie-making anxiety.

By 1990 he was a superstar, the most in demand actor of the decade. He'd proved himself to himself and, more importantly, to the father who had left home when he was just six years old. He was brought up to the belief that you can never be friends with your son.

Michael Douglas became an expert on women and was in no way inhibited in his performance to make Sharon Stone a star. But, like all his roles, it didn't help his marriage, which had been stretched over the years by work and the separations it caused. 'It's been very hard,' said Douglas, adding: 'I married Diandra when she was nineteen years old. She was not only going through a growing up process of her own, but she was married to this guy who was like this blitzkrieg – totally absorbed and obsessed by making movies.'

Majorca-born Diandra Douglas was actually twenty years old in 1977 when she attended the Inauguration party for President Jimmy Carter. Michael Douglas was bearded and long-haired after an eighteen-month globe-trotting carouse and booze-up with Jack Nicholson, who had won the Best Actor Oscar, playing the lead in *One Flew Over the Cuckoo's Nest*. Diandra had no idea who Michael Douglas was – she'd missed one hundred and four hours of television episodes of *The Streets of San Francisco* – and she didn't want to know. But he followed her and her date to a nightclub, and finally persuaded her to attend the next day's Inauguration ceremonies with him.

'She looked like a Botticelli madonna. I don't believe in reincarnation but I felt we'd met in a different life. There was a timelessness about her, as if she'd crossed many generations and qualities . . . It rained on Inauguration Day. We fled to my hotel room. I knew I had to change a lot of things if we were going to survive together. I owed Diandra a tremendous amount of time.

'She's been very patient. All I saw with my father was a tower of strength. My son Cameron and I have the ability to play, to be intimate. He tells me secrets. I think he sees my foibles and vulnerabilities a little more than I saw my father's. I'm a romantic at heart.'

And very aware of his body. He worked hard to get his face looking younger for the early scenes in *The War of the Roses* but, like Sharon Stone, he was acutely aware of how focused the cameras would be on his sensitive areas in *Basic Instinct*. The movie's director of photography Jan De Bont was told by both Douglas and Stone that they wanted to look their best naked. She remembers: 'I said you've heard horror stories about actresses – but they will be nothing if you see my cellulite in this movie.'

A more overwhelming concern was the situation of Michael Douglas' marriage. He admitted: 'I was concerned about making a movie like *Basic Instinct* at the time. It was no secret that our marriage had gone through difficult patches.'

Of course, the other big concern was how his son Cameron would cope with his father's on-screen sexual antics. Michael Douglas was acutely aware of the pressures of having a famous father: 'I'd seen my Dad as *Spartacus* and shooting it out with Wyatt Earp at the OK Corral – you don't get much larger than life than that!

'Cameron and I talked about it. I said: "Cameron, it's moviemaking: you do movies all the time, you shoot people with guns and they die – but they *don't* die." And he said: "Yeah, Dad, but they aren't real bullets and that's not real blood. But you are actually physically kissing somebody and you are actually nude with somebody."' Which was totally accurate.

'Michael has a very powerful sexuality and almost a dangerous edge to his sexuality,' said Sharon Stone, adding: 'He's one cool daddy. He was extremely protective, extremely chivalrous. He made sure I was protected at all times. When we had to do the parts of the sex scenes that were naughty naughty, he made a lot of jokes and was really warm . . . I started out wearing a crotch patch, but found I was comfortable enough to throw it away. I just took off my robe and went: "Let's all stop pretending, I'm nude, we all know it, let's go." Michael and I are the Ginger Rogers and Fred Astaire of the 1990s.'

Paul Verhoeven, overhearing this remark, observed: 'Right, the horizontal Fred Astaire and Ginger Rogers.'

'I've spent some quality time with her,' says Michael Douglas of Sharon Stone, happily adding: 'To create the illusion of the Fuck of the Century for ten or eleven hours a day over four or five days of shooting – I mean, you're exhausted!'

Energy-conservation involved the doing away with crotch pads. She and Michael Douglas agreed to work naked together. For Sharon Stone, it meant dispensing with a specially shaped, netted, moleskin G-string. She explained her artistic motivation: 'Every time you have to pee you have to unglue and reglue it, which is quite painful. Besides, Michael's a real professional and obviously there wasn't going to be anything untoward so I felt very safe. And, of course, there isn't anything sexy about doing sex scenes. Realistic sex scenes? Oh, it's incredibly realistic – it's clearly some male sex fantasy that the woman's gonna, like, jump down in the bed and have three orgasms in four minutes. You know, that's how it goes at my house . . . I think they should have cut to Michael at the end of the sex scene and he should have been smoking an entire pack of cigarettes, like twenty of them all around his mouth.'

Which brings us back to the director.

Verhoeven had his own difficulties with the sex scenes: 'I felt it was so goddamned difficult to do psychologically. The tension is so – I mean, taking your clothes off even if you have the set restricted to seven or eight people is still unpleasant. You, as the director, say: "And now you have to put yourself on top of each other. OK, let's start moving . . . OK, stick your tongue out – can you lick her? Can you lick her nipple a bit more? Or his nipple?" . . . I mean, you have to say it. It's awkward for everybody.'

But not too much for Michael Douglas. Verhoeven agrees: 'I think he knows about women. He's not afraid of women, *ja*? Some men are afraid and then it looks clumsy, but I think he feels OK with a woman.'

Or women. In November 1989, Michael Douglas, looking wearily sexy in classic superstar fashion, grey cashmere sweater, white cotton shirt, black cowboy boots, tight jeans (waist: 29ins; legs: 33ins) and smelling of Habit Rouge after-shave, had just watched *The War of the Roses*, the apocalyptic tale of divorce in which he co-starred with Kathleen Turner and was directed by long-time friend Danny DeVito.

It brought home the shock of divorce. 'Well, after seeing the end result of *The War of the Roses*, I'm definitely shaken up. It's only reconfirmed the fact that I am going home this afternoon.'

But after *Basic Instinct* he didn't stay home often enough.

Sharon Stone, who had and would continue to devote everything to her work, was also going to learn that hard and sometimes painful lesson.

13

The Flash

'When she took her knickers off she gave them to me
as a present'
    Paul Verhoeven, on a gift from Sharon Stone, 1992

Despite all the controversy and hyperbole in the summer of
1992, it is only with hindsight that those involved in *Basic
Instinct* realised that they were creating the first mainstream
multi-million dollar orgasm movie.

There was such intense prejudgment that it was probably
absurd even to imagine that the film would get a fair evalua-
tion. The expensive script, the protests during filming, the
wrangles over the rating, all are elements to upset critics and
possibly a film's box-office chances. Sharon Stone was doing
publicity for the film, but so was everyone else in the project.
As Sherry Lansing had said, that's how you become an international star – you go out and hustle.

Also, with hindsight, Stone's flash seems now so tame. But
there were gasps at the first international screening of the
movie at Tri-Star Pictures studios in west Los Angeles. How
far would this movie go?

From the moment she appears on screen, Sharon Stone's
Catherine Tramell is an eye-catcher. She has a French twist
hairdo and snow-white sheath with matching swing coat and
looks like a 1940s Hollywood movie star. Except for her short
skirts. She's the dark one of the movie, but dresses herself in

cream, white and smoke. There is no display of cleavage and her designs don't cling. Cleverly, they merely skim.

'Have you ever fucked on cocaine, Nick?' Stone's Catherine Tramell inquires of an anxious-looking Michael Douglas in the police interrogation room as she parts her legs, revealing glimpses of pubic hair.

Basic Instinct is a slickly made, chic, cosmetic film that pushes plenty of buttons. The $3 million basic premise is that Tramell, a $100 million heiress, writes novels that become true. They also give her an alibi. No one would write a novel about a murder and then kill, would they? Quickly, Michael Douglas doesn't care what risks he's taking to be with Tramell. He's 'The Shooter', the danger-loving cop who is happy to risk all for the Fuck of the Century. Douglas' confidence as Nick Curran, that arrogant swagger which his father also has, held the movie together. But it was Stone's playing of the cool blonde, the Grace Kelly ice princess who likes to indulge in all sorts of games, that remains the key to the movie.

By February 1991, the *Los Angeles Times* was featuring Stone in their movie 'Outtakes' column. And she was offering quotes on the sexual heat of the movie which was to begin filming a couple of months later: 'I know the more sensitive scenes will be handled with total integrity. The character is so complex, the nudity is not the role's greatest demand.'

Fourteen months later, Stone was accusing Verhoeven of tricking her into revealing everything. 'You could see all the way up to Nebraska,' she wailed about The Flash. Verhoeven is all over newspapers, denying he misrepresented himself to Stone. And she responds: 'He's a liar.'

This was in March and April of 1992 and Stone expanded: 'When I saw the movie I realised I had been betrayed in this one particular scene. I did the action believing it was going to be shot in a certain way. I was supposed to be shaded very dark. I now realise that was a very stupid thing to do on my part. I made a tremendous error of judgment. I never felt exploited by the director when I was making the film, but I certainly felt exploited when I watched it.

'That shot was there, despite the fact that I did not agree to it. I understand now that the people who turned it down probably did so because they knew they would have to face the music later.'

She was double-crossed, so to speak. But the tune changed as the box-office music got sweeter. And Sharon Stone became a star.

By late April 1992, she was saying The Flash was *her* idea. 'I wanted it to be alluded to, but not to get a bird's eye view.' Later that year, she appeared on the American late-night satire show *Saturday Night Live* and spoofed the scene: she did a comic commercial spot for 'Taster's Choice Spermicidal Jelly.' Yet, she still couldn't escape. Six gay activists were arrested for protesting at the NBC TV studios in New York for her 'perpetuation of anti-gay stereotypes'. A TV executive reported: 'She wasn't flustered by the protests or the heckling. She knew how to handle the situation and how to handle herself. She was a cool lady.'

Publicly, she remained hot about Verhoeven's 'trickery'. In an interview at that time, Michael Douglas said that his co-star felt she had been tricked. He put on Verhoeven's Dutch accent and said: 'The shot will be very dark. Shaded, very dark.'

Verhoeven himself was quizzed about his relationship with Stone at that time and replied: '*Ja*, Sharon is Catherine without killing. That's a quote, isn't it?'

Well, maybe.

Verhoeven takes full credit for The Flash. It was his idea. He orchestrated it and now says: 'It's a great scene. Sharon was wrong to criticise it. I know she complained to me and I said: "You saw that shot and you agreed it was fine."

'When she took her knickers off she gave them to me as a present. And then I found myself in the strange position of having to defend myself.' And he clearly enjoys doing so.

Verhoeven says the other actresses who were up for the Stone role did not take it 'because of the explicitness of the sex. Michael wanted Isabelle Adjani, but she refused after reading the script. I told all the actresses we interviewed how I wanted it to go. I did not want them to sign a contact and then have big discussions about whether they would bare their breasts – yes or no – and for how many seconds.'

Stone is adamant about the extent of The Flash: 'He told me I had to take off my white underwear because the light was reflecting off it. He assured me that the scene was so shadowy that you wouldn't see anything. I did that action believing it was going to be shot in a certain way.'

Verhoeven is equally insistent about what he intended to do in the movie: 'I did this because I like sex. This is a very simple and honest answer. I like to portray sex. There are a lot of things you can say through sex, as it is the most direct communication system in the world. I've always been irritated by the fact that we're not supposed to show sex. I've always felt compelled to attack it. You can only justify sex scenes with plot. All the sex is related to plot. You cannot get away with sex as an ornament – people would have stopped coming to see the film. *Basic Instinct* is a thriller and there is great sexual and psychological tension running throughout the scenes which make them work. Things will change in the 1990s – male nudity will be in mainstream films – that's always been a double standard. I think all sexuality should be opened up and taken out of the dark corner. That's what I try to do.'

With some passion. And not just heterosexual sex.

Catherine Tramell and her lesbian lover have a longing kiss which is aimed, on Tramell's part, to get Michael Douglas going. 'I wanted a scene that wasn't some sick male fantasy but an example of people who live together and are in love as in "I want to smell your skin, look into your eyes, taste the way you taste",' said Stone, adding: 'Too many times, homosexual love scenes in film or theatre are done in safe, unrealistic ways. So when Paul said he'd test anybody, I thought it would be good if I sent in my best friend Mimi Craven. If you're going to do a lesbian love scene, why not do it with your best friend? . . . Later, when Paul showed me the film tapes of three other girls and I saw Leilani, I said: "That girl's hot!"'

So, Leilani Sarelle, a dark-haired sultry beauty, won the lesbian lover role. 'The first day we were supposed to shoot the scene every crew member I had ever seen before showed up on the set. Leilani's boyfriend was there too and I said: "Any tips you'd like to impart before we roll?" And he did. Leilani and I had a very personal, very deep trust. I mean, I really love that girl and I feel that girl really loves me.'

Crew members on the film claim that Stone got so excited during filming that the film set had to be closed down to stop her getting *totally* carried away. The disco scene in the film involved more than four hundred extras. There was talk of drugs, including Ecstasy, being passed around by the extras as they thumped up and down on the disco floor.

One of the actors on the set said: 'In an early part of the scene Sharon has to fondle another woman as part of a come-on to Michael Douglas. Paul Verhoeven insisted that she moved her hands further up this other girl's skirt. Each time they shot a take, Paul would yell: "Cut!" Then he would tell Sharon to put her hands higher up the girl's thighs. By the end, her hands were all the way up the inside of the other girl's legs. And Sharon was really sweating and had a glazed, sexually excited look in her eyes. It was no wonder they were so hot. They must have done thirty takes. At the end, Sharon and the girl were hugging and kissing each other.

'And when Michael Douglas got into the act it was like a porno flick. Sharon had to gyrate on his groin and she was doing it really sexually. Then she kissed him deeply on the mouth and we could all see just how far her tongue was going. Michael seemed perfectly happy to take it all from her. Then Sharon asked Paul if she could take a break – she wanted to cool down. She looked like she might rape him there and then.'

Other actors/extras on the film say that, during filming of the disco sequence, couples were actually having sex. 'There was one gal in this super-slinky dress going at it with the guy. During a break I found out why they were so heated up. He came and offered me Ecstasy. They were obviously doing it. And there was the smell of marijuana coming from the restrooms. When the film started again the same couple were in a corner behind some cameras having sex. The woman had her dress pulled all the way up and her bottom was buck naked.

'The director, Paul, was telling everyone on the dance floor to change partners and imagine we were on blind dates with people. Some of the amateurs, extras who had just come in off the streets, got really carried away. They were fondling each other intimately as they danced.'

Sharon Stone says she told Verhoeven: 'As this script has all these nude and sex scenes, if this is going to be Evian water on various body parts under blue light in slow motion, I can't do it. I'd feel like an asshole. If we're going to do *real* sex – exciting, voyeuristic, funny, stupid, clumsy, thrilling – I'm willing to take the risk with you, for you, because I believe in you. I don't thrive on being naked at every possible moment but it's not the biggest deal in the world to me.'

'When Paul showed me the storyboards, I said: "Jesus Christ, I'm going to be sitting on my shins." I not only have to do a complete backbend but I also have to pull myself back up without using my hands. And then make it look as if I'm getting off. This athletic feat took a lot of work. It took some training to get my quadriceps strong enough so that I could manage it. I also had to be flexible enough to be able to do it fifty billion times so we could do all the takes. I got embarrassed but not very often – that's just the kind of roguish girl I am.

'This was embarrassing. In my first movies explicit sex

scenes were scarier. We were getting ready to do a take and Michael put his cappuccino down on the side of the bed – not the camera side. At the last second I took off my robe, tossed it over the side of the bed and heard the cappuccino fall over onto the white carpeting. Forgetting that I was meant to be behaving like a movie star and not some middle-class girl from Pennsylvania, I leapt over the side of the bed, screaming: "Oh, My God!" Only then did I realise that everybody in the room knows me better than my gynaecologist does. I was just horrified because I literally dove off the side of the bed. But you know what? We've all got the same stuff – I don't know what the big deal is, really. Sex is a mystery I don't possess. My image is manufactured from very little. As a teen I was a geek and at eighteen I found self-esteem. I realised I could create an event – this more attractive woman.'

Costume designer Ellen Mirojnick designed Catherine Tramell's scene-stealing police interrogation dress and coat ensemble, as well as her exciting disco outfit, a coppery beaded cowl-neck dress with a dipping back. The character's other outfits were picked out from a range of Los Angeles department stores including Fred Segal, Saks Fifth Avenue and Hermès, where Tramell's white cashmere throw, as well as the white bee-patterned silk Jacquard man's tuxedo scarf found at the murder scene. (They sell for $195 at Hermès on Rodeo Drive in Beverly Hills.) Barry Kieselstein-Cord designed all the jewelry exotically displayed by Sharon Stone. Her co-star got most of his clothes from Nino Cerutti.

'I could see the dangers in Michael,' says Sharon Stone. 'How you work *sooooo* hard and just keep going for the best. There's pressure and it's tough.'

Jeanne Tripplehorn, who played Tom Cruise's wife in *The Firm* was a classically trained actress when she made her film debut in *Basic Instinct*. Her call-sheet listed twelve pairs of cutaway underpants with Velcro so they could be ripped open more easily. 'Stunt undies! And make-up for bruises.'

Tripplehorn, who after the film was nicknamed

'Trippleporn,' plays Beth Gardner, the police psychologist and lover of Michael Douglas' Nick. But is she what she seems? It was the couple's date-rape encounter which enraged San Francisco's lesbian community. She says: 'It was a rough sex scene between two consenting adults. That's what we always called it. I call it the perks of the business.'

Accustomed to the New York stage, a Juilliard acting college graduate, this was her big break in the movies. Almost literally. With a Hollywood sound stage doubling as Beth Gardner's apartment, she had several rehearsals with Verhoeven directing her and Douglas going into her apartment and making urgent love. She recalls every word of Michael Douglas' whispered instructions as they filmed one of the film's early erotic scenes – a preparation for the Sharon Stone sex moments.

'He said: "OK, throw you against the wall. Kiss kiss kiss. Leg up. Kiss kiss kiss. Up against the next wall. Hands on the back of my neck. Kiss kiss kiss. Hands over my head. Now scoop you up. Into the next room. Over the back of the chair. Face in the pillow."

'When the cameras rolled it was like a rodeo. It worked because we had those physical signposts to hit and we could just be spontaneous, move around, and fill it with intensity and emotion. In the first take my bra popped open – that was a big surprise and it actually heightened the scene. When we did it we were passionate and the bra went open and we didn't stop. Michael makes you feel at ease. Sharon and I both felt more comfortable because it was him. But it was intense. Michael had to bite the back of my neck according to the script, and after three takes I said to him: "You can really bite me." He said: "I am biting you." But I couldn't feel it – that's how involved we were. The next day the make-up people had to cover the bruises.'

Michael Douglas was in for a different sort of bruising. After his wife walked in on his sexual encounter at the Regent Beverly Wilshire Hotel in Beverly Hills – and *Basic Instinct* had made him an even greater star than before – he was given an ultimatum by Diandra. Get help! And as a result, he ordered a private jet and, at 5.56 p.m. on 15 September 1992, arrived at the famous Sierra Tucson Clinic in Arizona, looking, said staff, 'very depressed and dishevelled'.

For the next thirty days he stayed at the clinic which helps patients cope with addictions of all kinds. He was treated for his self-confessed addictions to sex, drink and drugs. At the clinic Douglas, a late starter as a Hollywood sex symbol, said he had 'obsessive' sexual fantasies. He told doctors he desperately wanted to overcome his chemical and sexual addictions, otherwise he faced losing 'a wife and a little boy I love very much'. The treatment cost him more than money.

If he had to let it 'all hang out' in *Basic Instinct* with Sharon Stone, he had to do even more at the clinic. Patients were seen for two and a half hours each day in group therapy sessions at the pink-painted adobe style desert 'resort'. A fellow patient said Douglas 'dropped one bombshell after another' during the therapeutic counselling.

'Sex is just a wave that sweeps over me – the impulse, that is. It's compulsive. Overpowering. And when the urge comes I'm hopeless – every time. I've even run the most incredible, stupid risks. The consequences are the loss of my marriage. And possible disease.'

Former patients claimed he said that his wife Diandra had stopped having sexual relations with him following the hotel incident. He said: 'She was totally repulsed. There's been no intimacy since then. She told me: "You bastard – now you could give me AIDS. But you won't. You won't get the chance."'

During one therapy session, Douglas said: 'I've got a wife and a little boy. I love them very much. I'm here because I'm destroying myself. And I'm destroying them.'

Patients and staff at the clinic have said on record that Douglas said he had cheated on his wife with high-class call-girls and had taunted his wife with his affairs. He also said he has used cocaine for twenty years and was a 'mean' drunk. One report ran: 'Michael explained that the inner demons took over. He just said he was driven to want other women than his wife. On occasions with prostitutes he hadn't worn a condom.'

At one therapy session he said: '*Basic Instinct*? I'm a basic misfit. I was at rock bottom. I felt like a rat. What a joke! I smoke one joint daily and since 1970 I have snorted cocaine. There's been LSD, Ecstasy, PCP and mushrooms. Then there's the booze. Vodka. Daily. In a social setting, usually more than I anticipate. At home and with close friends I can control it. I feel lonely and confused. Emotionally numb – I lost my wife's trust. I lost my wife's respect. I feel sad. I feel guilty.'

The superstar was quizzed by counsellors about his sex addiction. He was asked to give a point-blank 'yes' or 'no' to the type of sexual behaviour he wanted or had been involved in. He replied 'No, ma'am' to pornography, voyeurism, cross-dressing, violent and dangerous sex. He also denied ever taking part in incest or child sex abuse or making obscene phone calls. Asked about affairs with women, he said 'Yes.'

He checked into the clinic using the name Mike Morrell and gave as contacts his wife and Dr Michael Horowitz who, as well as being a doctor for Elizabeth Taylor, is the director of substance abuse at Cedars-Sinai Medical Centre in Los Angeles. Despite Douglas' famous face, the clinic ran a credit check on him. He chose to 'self-pay' with a $6,000 deposit.

The treatment involved mostly intensive and sometimes intensively embarrassing group therapies, as well as a first four-day cold-turkey 'detox'. By October 1992, Michael and Diandra Douglas were a public couple again, attending award ceremonies in Los Angeles and New York.

During the sessions at the Arizona clinic Douglas blamed the pressure of his career for leading him astray. 'No one understands the long hours, the demands. A large part of me believes in the work ethic. I work really hard to provide and keep things going and I'm sure my wife bitches at how much

I'm working. I know how difficult it is for ladies who do not have a career per se, in terms of discovering who they are and their own identity – and in other times in my life, in other relationships, I've dealt with that. But I don't have a lot of patience for it. I've always felt like I'm working hard, providing, making a good home, a good life for everybody, which is not to be sneered at.'

But that wasn't all Sharon Stone wanted. Suddenly, after all the waiting, all the years, she was the toast of Hollywood. And the joke was that it happened in a flash. Could she cope with it?

14

Superstar

'Since becoming famous I get to torture a better class of man'

Sharon Stone, 1993

American comedian Richard Lewis is convinced Sharon Stone can cope with anything. He is a member of the St James's Club on Sunset Boulevard, an art deco tower remodelled to cater for the very rich and famous. It has a gym where Lewis works out – and so does Sharon Stone. Which Lewis found out one afternoon: 'I'm on the Exercycle and there are two ladies well into the four-hundred-pound category on the treadmills. Anyway, out of the blue bursts in this meteorite – that's the feminine for meteor. I've been with a lot of actresses but she makes Sean Young and Debra Winger look like Mother Teresa's disciples. Her energy outdistances them all. She might as well wear a placard around her neck that says BEWARE!

'She zooms in and she's remarkably beautiful and very thin and she starts doing her stretching. And while she's stretching she's talking about the last few days of lovemaking. I'm sitting there, listening, astonished by her bravado. To me it wasn't rude but amazing how she revealed such intimate things to strangers. Explicit terms about lovemaking and questions like: "Why did I do it? I should never have gone back with him. I never should have slept with him!" I listened to every detail of this beautiful woman's sex life and it got me horny enough to leave the gym. I darted to a pay phone. I mean I had to get laid after this conversation. My feeling is I could just stand alongside her and listen to her talk about her sex life once in a while and I would never have to date again. That would be plenty for me.'

Sharon Stone made many other people feel the same way, including Robert Evans, who had once been one of the biggest players in Hollywood. But how did *she* feel?

'Suddenly being famous is exhilarating but when I realised it wasn't going away it became scary and claustrophobic. Fame is a weird thing. When you get famous – I think Cary Grant said it best – it's not so much you that changes, but the people around you. People lose the reality that you're human, that your feelings can be hurt, that you feel insecure. You're perceived as something different than human – what it is, I have yet to discover.

'I had an enormous amount of power in terms of creating the character in *Basic Instinct* because by interpreting Joe Eszterhas' material and incorporating Paul's direction I made her up. I created her . . . But the love scenes were all story-boarded out, choreographed like dance sequences. The entire movie was incredibly corny and all from the position of a fantasy. But I got labelled as this sex symbol – which seems a peculiar label to begin with – so that the next time out I wanted to portray sexuality that seemed more compassionate.'

She chose *Sliver* which was another screenplay from the word processor of Joe Eszterhas, but with a plot from the rather more complex brain of the brilliant novelist Ira Levin. By then, Sharon Stone had decided to play the Mae West of the 1990s. She says she's not an actress in the emotive Meryl Streep sense and she's also not a classic beauty like Isabella Rossellini or a pouting sex kitten like Bardot or a patrician wonder like Audrey Hepburn.

She created Sharon Stone. It is quite an act.

She became a reminder of the difference between eroticism

and exhibitionism. One can exhilarate, while the other might simply exhaust. Sharon Stone surprises. By shedding her clothes and her inhibitions she achieved controversial stardom – she was *the* new full-figured look. Stone, like a new Malibu restaurant, became the item of the moment. The restaurant was reviewed in the *Los Angeles Times* and the article ended: 'Jackets not required but breast implants preferred.'

Sharon Stone already had everything *she* needed. Jane Fonda had an aerobic body, like most of the celluloid crowd of the 1970s and 1980s, but she was out of the shape that Hollywood wanted when Sharon Stone arrived. It wasn't sexism. It was business. It was what audiences wanted to pay for. Sharon Stone thrashing around in silk sheets with her naked derrière in the air and Michael Douglas writhing happily below was what was wanted.

And Robert Evans wanted a big box-office hit.

He had the hot young actor Billy Baldwin, enjoying the success of the firefighter-thriller movie *Backdraft* and brother of Alec Baldwin (who became Mr Kim Basinger in 1994), and he wanted Sharon Stone. Badly.

She wasn't interested. At first.

She told a friend: 'I'm right on time.' Like Michael Douglas, she had always believed her success would arrive late but 'on time'. Her best friend Mimi Craven said: 'Sharon was always convinced it would happen for her. It was just a matter of time. I don't think there was any arrogance in that attitude, other than if you work hard enough for something it *should* happen. And she'd had the experience not to make mistakes when it did. She could use her life in films to help her. She's a bright girl at any time but when she has to deal in business she's super-sharp.'

'Even though some things have been rough and it's been a long haul it's certainly given me the opportunity to refocus my goals. I feel I've been lucky. I've been on time,' says Stone.

Part of that timing was her performance in John

Frankenheimer's *Year of the Gun*. It was released in American cinemas in November 1991, and suddenly gave her some gravitas. *Year of the Gun* is set in Rome of 1978, when Italy was being terrorised by the Red Brigade, an ultra-left-wing bunch of hoodlums intent on taking down the government. Knee-cappings and kidnappings were the terrorist menu as Italy was stunned and stopped in fear of the next major incident.

Sharon Stone played an aggressive American photographer, Alison King, who was determined to infiltrate the Red Brigade. She becomes convinced that David Raybourne (Andrew McCarthy), another American working for an English language paper, can help her. He's not interested. But Stone's Alison gets them both involved in a nasty web of deceit and violence.

What gave Sharon Stone the edge in the film was that, as a nineteen-year-old model, she was working in Rome during the Red Brigade's reign of terror. 'It was really scary. There was this kind of intensity everywhere. It's such a small country that everybody feels politically involved or active. So the points of view are more personal than the points of view of an American. Italy is the size of an American state – we don't think about that when we think of another country. The politics were only meant to be a backdrop to the story.'

Stone, who had her first taste of pasta when she was seventeen, had little knowledge of Italy until she went there to model. But by the time of *Year of the Gun* she was an expert: 'I knew then that you had to use all your experiences to put some proper muscle on the screen.'

In 1994, Ron Reyer, then the principal of Saegertown High School, where Sharon Stone had been a self-confessed 'geek', said that he had to keep his one remaining copy of the school's 1975 yearbook under lock and key. The yearbook contains two early photographs of Sharon Stone which sell for $100 each. 'I have to keep my copy locked in the safe,' said Reyer, adding: 'We don't dare leave it in the school library.

This is the most important student on earth. She's done so much for us in telling about serious education – about trying to do your best. She was an exceptional student and she's gone on to Hollywood, but it's her mind that has helped her achieve all of her ambitions. Hey, she looks great and has lots of talent, but at the end of the day it is your mind that will make you a winner . . . You've heard about mind over matter?'

Sharon Stone was a bona fide superstar when *Sliver* went into production towards the end of 1992. The film's producer Robert Evans was one of Tinseltown's wonderful mavericks. 'If there's anything Hollywood wants out of Robert Evans, it's to see him fail,' *Life* magazine reported in 1969.

The first time Ernest Hemingway met Robert Evans, in 1957, he didn't like him. Evans was then a clothes manufacturer but had become an actor to play Pedro Romero in the film of Hemingway's *The Sun Also Rises*. Hemingway found Darryl Zanuck, who was producing the film as the boss of 20th Century-Fox Film Studios, and demanded that Evans be sacked. Zanuck flew from Hollywood to Mexico City and told Evans to get into his bullfighter's costume and appear in the bullring. Over a loudspeaker system Zanuck announced: 'The kid stays in the picture. And anybody who doesn't like it can leave.'

Nobody left. For the next three decades, Robert Evans was Hollywood news. He married. His wives were actresses Sharon Hugueny, Camilla Sparv, Ali MacGraw and Phyllis George. His deals were legendary. And so were his women and his parties. And by 1992, after a long spell in the Hollywood wilderness, he desperately wanted more Hollywood success.

Evans survived in the Hollywood environment first as an actor, then as a studio executive and then as an independent producer. It cost him a lot. He had that electric switch charm – flip it on, flip it off. He was boss of Paramount Studios for seven years, which was a longer tenure than the six years of his four marriages. He is the ultimate Hollywood person, a close friend of Jack Nicholson, Warren Beatty and Roman Polanski. Beatty once wanted to buy the film rights to F. Scott Fitzgerald's *The Great Gatsby* and star Robert Evans in the title role. That was in the 1970s. In the 1990s, both men still think – rightly – that it was a good idea; both have been disdained at times for being too handsome. When Beatty's movie *Reds* failed to blockbuster the Oscars in 1984, Beatty – who had won as Best Director – turned to Evans, and said: 'You and I, Bob, will never get the sympathy vote.' Beatty said: 'Bob Evans is a star-maker and in Sharon Stone he saw one of the biggest stars of his career. He felt he could make a film and a personality take off at the same time. It would be an over-whelming comeback.'

And Robert Evans, with great pride, conned Sharon Stone into starring in *Sliver*. Evans, with that perpetual suntan, is amazingly amusing about how circumstances can change.

Once the chief executive – the man who said yes or no to movies at Paramount Studios – in 1993, he was a nonentity. Not only unable to get an idea through the famous pewter-coloured concrete tower-shaped gates of Paramount Studios, he couldn't get a drive-on pink visitor's pass.

Evans, once one of the most sought-after producers in the world, said that in 1989: 'I was so cold – I had a *disease*! Everything was going against me. I had no deal at Paramount. I had no deal anywhere. I couldn't make a deal if I had Dustin Hoffman, Al Pacino, Warren Beatty, Jack Nicholson, a script by William Goldman and William Shakespeare and everyone willing to work for nothing – they weren't interested. Then I get a call one afternoon from an agent who says if I want to get back into business I have to read this book. It's *Sliver* by Ira Levin.' Then, the words you really never should say in Hollywood: 'If we don't fuck it up in the making, we have ourselves something that people have never seen before.'

Of course, they did. *Sliver* was a mess, but it was an inter-national success because of Sharon Stone. Evans had known he needed her, needed an ace, and by now that's what Stone was. Nevertheless, she had never encountered a character like Bob Evans. Evans, who was 64 in 1994, when his auto-biography *The Kid Stays in the Picture* was published, arrived in Hollywood in 1954 as a B-movie actor in films like *Man Of A Thousand Faces*, *The Fiend Who Walked The West* and *The Sun Also Rises*. He moved on with charm and daring, becoming vice president in charge of film production at Paramount Studios. He was responsible for hits like Jane Fonda and Robert Redford's *Barefoot in the Park*, *The Odd Couple* with Jack Lemmon and Walter Matthau, the first two *Godfather* films, *Chinatown*, with his great friends Jack Nicholson and Roman Polanski, and *Love Story*. He married Ali MacGraw following *Love Story* and they have a son Josh, who is now also a Hollywood producer. Ali MacGraw ran off with Steve McQueen after they filmed the aptly named *The Getaway* in 1972 – a year after her greatest success opposite Ryan O'Neal in Evans' *Love Story*.

Bob Evans was Hollywood for a time. He would have Henry Kissinger over for a premiere or Ted Kennedy for a set of tennis. There is the story that once he asked the girl he was seeing who her favourite actor was. She said Cary Grant. Did she have another favourite? Yes, Douglas Fairbanks Junior. When she turned up at Evans' house for dinner that night, Grant was seated on her right and Fairbanks on her left. They said it wouldn't last. It didn't.

In 1980, Evans was convicted of possession of cocaine, which doesn't sound such a great shock in the scheme of things, but it began Bob Evans' decline. He spent six years producing *The Cotton Club*, which was a mammoth disaster. He was going to co-star with his friend Jack Nicholson in *The Two Jakes*, the sequel to his marvellous success *Chinatown*, but was 'let go' from that failed attempt in 1985. And, after twenty-one years, he was asked to leave his offices at Paramount Studios. He had lost a fortune through the failure of the gangster/jazz age movie *The Cotton Club*, but in 1990 his reputation was also in tatters, after a former girlfriend was indicted for the murder of Roy Radin, another *Cotton Club* producer. Evans was questioned by police, and for months believed he might also be indicted for murder. They were miserable months for the man who took over Paramount Studios when it was in danger of being closed down. By the time Evans left, it was the number one film studio in Hollywood, following hits like *The Godfather*, *The Conversation* and *Rosemary's Baby*.

Rosemary's Baby was to be the key to Evans' comeback attempt; and would introduce Sharon Stone to her future lover. In 1988, Evans started a production company with William Macdonald, who was then thirty-four years old. Macdonald was a law school graduate with experience in international finance. He had attempted to produce his own films, including one based on Richard Condon's novel *Prizzi's Family*, the prequel to *Prizzi's Honor*, which had been a huge movie success for Jack Nicholson and Anjelica Huston. But it wasn't easy.

'There aren't that many people in this town with the depth of knowledge, the ability to make the product. I wanted to find the right person,' said Macdonald.

Enter Robert Evans, the producer of Macdonald's favourite movie, *Chinatown*. Macdonald brought in two friends, Lawrence Giesen, a corporate banker, and Ariel Wapnir, who had worked with him on the development of the *Prizzi's Family* film, and together they formed The Robert Evans Film Company.

Then, the jinx: the Roy Radin case became headlines, with a string of arrests. But Macdonald and his friends stayed with Evans. 'We all sat back,' says Macdonald, 'and said: "We can make it through this but it's going to take all our energy, and we are going to have to be as keen-witted and clear-headed as anybody and even more so. And we've got to make this company look like the IBM of the movie business."'

Bob Evans was to concentrate on the big-budget films,

while his partners established the company. And Evans had been called about *Sliver*. He became obsessed with it. 'For one year, I romanced the *Sliver* book. Warners read it, 20th Century-Fox read it, Universal read it and they're all bidding and Ira Levin doesn't want to hear an offer. He said he had an emotional connection to the property and he just didn't want to let it go. The only movie adaptation that he thought was better than the novel that he wrote was *Rosemary's Baby*, and he would only do it if Roman Polanski would direct it, so I sort of gave up hope. And then Warren Beatty calls me one day and says: "Why don't you send him Roman's book, *Roman by Polanski*, because in the book Roman talks about how much you had to do with making *Rosemary's Baby*."

'So I sent Ira Levin the book and he calls me and says: "Gee, Bob, I never knew you had that much to do with the film – you can have the book for any price you want." Now, when other studios were willing to pay one and a half million dollars for it, we got it for one quarter of a million dollars.'

The price, more accurately, was nearer half a million dollars. Nevertheless, Evans had done a good deal. And, he says, he did another one with Joe Eszterhas. Evans said: 'Joe says: "Listen, motherfucker, I've wanted to work with you for the past twenty years – I read about you when I was a newspaper man in Cleveland. You're not a bullshitter. You're not afraid to go in there and you're not an accountant. I'll do my first adaptation for you and forget the numbers on it."'

So, Evans had a book about murder and voyeurism and masturbation, and a screenwriter who had more than proved his skills at the sharp end of such raw material. What he needed now was a leading lady.

By then, everybody in Hollywood wanted to be in bed with Sharon Stone. She was top of the most wanted list, ahead of Julia Roberts, Michelle Pfeiffer and Geena Davis. She was getting twelve 'firm' film offers a month – most A-list actresses would be more than happy with half that number. Her looks and luck and attitude had bewitched Hollywood. One studio executive said she was the female equivalent of Arnold Schwarzenegger – transcending the sex-bomb image the way he had surpassed his image as simply a muscle man. 'If Sharon makes the right moves – and the right movies – she's going to be one of this century's sensations. She's got it all going for her. She's not some kid who just got off a Greyhound bus and made it. The industry admires her for paying her dues.'

'The key to her image is that she's a force of her own,' said producer Robert Lawrence, adding: 'That's what people saw in *Basic Instinct* and that's why she's riding on the top.'

But all Robert Evans wanted was a star. He was told Sharon Stone's name on *Sliver* would guarantee $75 million at the box-office.

She wasn't interested. 'There was a big problem with Sharon,' says Evans, explaining: 'It had nothing to do with money. She was afraid of doing "Basic Instinct 2", and we all spoke to her and couldn't change her mind. Joe Eszterhas tried and I even went to her drama coach and tried to convince her, but she worked against me and told her not to do it. I told her that Demi Moore was desperate to do it and Bruce Willis was willing to do the male lead for nothing, just so Demi would get it. It still didn't interest her. She wouldn't do it . . . We had two days left before we had to re-cast or lose the picture and I tried my last shot on her. I said: "Geena Davis is in make-up, starting Monday."

'*That* got her. Suddenly she got anxious to do the picture . . . Of course, Geena had never read it. I never sent it to her. Demi Moore was made up too. Everything was made up. When a starlet becomes a star they're just so worried about their next picture, and the only thing that got her to do it was that Geena Davis was going to do it and she'd been offered the *Basic Instinct* role before Sharon, so she didn't want Geena to have it. I'm just giving the honest way it happened.'

All the manipulation and games didn't do anybody much good – except Sharon Stone. *Sliver* proved that people wanted to go and see her, even in a troubled and confusing film. And that was all the endorsement she needed.

15

Sizzling

'Me and the rest of the world have already seen it and
it's no big deal'
 – Actor Billy Baldwin to Sharon Stone during the
production of *Sliver*, 1992, about the scene in which
she removes her underwear

Sharon Stone and her *Sliver* co-star Billy Baldwin hated each
other. She was the hottest leading lady in the world and it was
clear she intimidated Baldwin, younger brother of Alec
Baldwin, who married another Stone rival, Kim Basinger, in
1993. There was a lot rolling on this $50 million movie dice.
Sharon Stone wanted to prove she was as good as she said she
was. Robert Evans wanted resurrection. Billy Baldwin wanted
stardom, and the director, the Australian Phillip Noyce, who
had directed Harrison Ford's hit *Patriot Games* for Paramount
Studios, wanted to increase his highly professional visibility
in Hollywood.

In Hollywood everyone wants something. Which is why
you get the problems. It's all take.

'It was a difficult and confusing time for me,' says Sharon
Stone, adding: 'You are pulled in so many directions it really
is impossible to know which one to choose.'

But she chose the seemingly commercial road. Joe Eszterhas
had a track record of hits. And so did Robert Evans. Noyce
was a big A-list director, just off the action movie version of
novelist Tom Clancy's *Patriot Games*. What could go wrong?

Charisma is what soured the pot. Sharon Stone and Billy
Baldwin are just not believable as a sex machine couple in

Sliver. Stone and Michael Douglas – now there's a couple – it works.

Phillip Noyce – and, more importantly, Sherry Lansing at Paramount, who made *Sliver* her important first project when she took over as head of the studio in 1991 – had problems. *Sliver* didn't work.

'Sharon and Billy loathed each other and that's where all the problems were,' said a member of the production crew who filmed the 'sizzling' scenes between the two actors. Stone, as a recently divorced book editor, moves into an apartment building in New York – one of these slimline buildings in Manhattan, just a sliver – and finds that the previous occupant of her new home fell or was pushed from her balcony.

But by whom? The movie turns up suspects Tom Berenger as Jack Lansford, a Frederick Forsyth-style novelist with writer's block, and Baldwin as the young and charming Zeke Hawkins, the owner of the *Sliver* skyscraper and a grand voyeur. The implausibilities in the film go on and on.

And Sharon Stone's greatest regret was doing a replay of her *Basic Instinct* attention-grabber – taking off her knickers in a sequence where she's out having dinner in a smart restaurant with Baldwin. For the actress, as Robert Evans said, who didn't want to do 'Basic Instinct 2' it appeared absurd. It was absurd. But the pressure was on to make a 'hot' follow-up to *Basic Instinct* and, she admitted: 'You just get caught up in the wave of events.'

Billy Baldwin, like his brothers, believes he is above such issues. This was not a match-making in movie magic heaven. *Sliver* began filming in the autumn of 1992 and was to go on into the end of February the next year.

There were lots of sex scenes. Lots of voyeurism. But not lots of excitement. Despite this, Phillip Noyce had to – like Paul Verhoeven in *Basic Instinct* – clip away in the editing room to avoid a NC-17 rating. The rows went on and on between Noyce and Paramount Studios and the MPAA.

But that was after Noyce had made the movie. 'Thin lips, OK breath,' is how Baldwin described Sharon Stone after one of their first screen sexual encounters. Relations didn't get any better. 'I went out on a date with him and didn't want to kiss him goodnight,' Stone complained to Robert Evans. Baldwin remembers the evening and claims: 'I didn't even try to kiss her.'

These were not happy times for Sharon Stone. One day during filming she ran over to Billy Baldwin's camper truck and banged on his door. He was on the telephone to his girl-friend, the singer Chynna Phillips. 'She accused him of keeping everyone waiting,' said a crew member, adding: 'Billy spent twenty minutes more on the phone. Later, when Billy fluffed a line, Sharon turned and shouted to everyone on the set: "See, this is what I've got to work with!" Honestly, they *loathed* each other.'

Baldwin was not cowed. On the day they filmed the remarkably silly scene in which Stone takes off her panties in a restaurant and, in some strange pact of trust, hands them over to Baldwin, she was nervous. It was a little too close to the *Basic Instinct* flash and Baldwin took advantage of that. With everyone on the film set, he said: 'Me and the rest of the world have already seen it and it's no big deal.'

Baldwin, who was twenty-nine when he made the film in 1992, probably had much to regret. Sharon Stone looks spec-tacular in close-up, and if there are close-ups of the lady that means there is film of him on the editing floor.

'The editors were using the scenes of Sharon in close-up and that forced them to push Billy out of her scenes,' said Robert Evans. Was this a problem for her? Evans replied: 'No. She has balls like Mike Tyson.'

But that wasn't what she was selling or what was selling Sharon Stone. *Sliver* was to have more problems. And not just with the icy relationship between Stone and Baldwin. Joe Eszterhas' original ending involved helicopters, Hawaii and a volcano. Neither he nor anyone else has explained why. But in

November 1992, a second film unit was sent out into the Pacific and to the Hawaiian islands to film the final scenes. They involved Stone and Baldwin, but the actors were not needed for the second unit filming . . . which was lucky for them. The main helicopter crashed into the Kilauea volcano. Luckily pilot Craig Hosking, cinematographer Michael Benson and technician Chris Duddy amazingly survived. Hosking was able to radio for help and, although the trio spent a nasty night waiting over a pool of steaming lava, they got out with the film footage they needed.

The main problem however was that Sharon Stone and Billy Baldwin were not as steamy as the lava. *Sliver* was given a 'test' screening – a hand-picked public audience is invited to see the film for free, in return for filling in cards with their opinion – and Robert Evans' dream of a triumphant return to Hollywood fame seemed in trouble. The 'test' audiences liked Sharon Stone but thought the sex scenes, although 'pretty steamy', were 'juvenile'. One card said: 'It's like some high school scholar writing on the walls of a locker room.'

But The End was a bigger problem. As written by Joe Eszterhas, it had Stone and Baldwin unbuckling their seat belts as they flew into a volcano. Then the screen went blank and the moviegoers did not know if the couple they had spent the last 136 minutes with lived or died.

In the original script, Baldwin is both Sharon Stone's lover and the killer. 'Test' audiences didn't like the fact that he apparently got away with murder.

'I never thought the first ending could work,' says Robert Evans, adding: 'Audiences resented, and rightly so, the fact that in essence the killer got away without being caught.'

The *Sliver* team came up with five new endings. Joe Eszterhas, at his professional best, bashed out fifty-seven new pages of script in three days. And then he said: 'They can fuck with it now for all I care.' There were outside problems as well for Eszterhas to concern himself about, because, by then real-life marriages and love-lives had become as confused as the *Sliver* plot. After a run of short romance in Hollywood, Stone began an affair with Bill Macdonald from the Robert Evans Company, and Bill Macdonald's wife had become involved with Joe Eszterhas. The loser, it appeared, in this sexual merry-go-round seemed to be Eszterhas' wife (of twenty-four years in 1993) Geri.

On 3 May 1993, when the musical beds became public, Naomi Macdonald had been married to Bill for five months. That day she filed for annulment and he filed for divorce. They had been a couple for ten years and married in a Catholic ceremony in Rome. On Sunday, 2 May 1993, Eszterhas and Naomi Macdonald flew to Ohio to meet her parents.

The screenwriter and his wife had gone on holiday in Hawaii with Bill and Naomi Macdonald in January of 1992. Eighteen months later, Eszterhas was bragging that he had introduced Bill Macdonald to Sharon Stone 'to have Naomi for myself'. Eszterhas says: 'There was nothing romantic during our time in Hawaii, but things change.' He acknowledged that there was 'a circle of pain' because Naomi Macdonald and his wife 'had been best friends'.

Shortly after those two couples had been happily in Hawaii, Sharon Stone, who was baptised a Catholic, was attending the Oscars in Los Angeles with Country and Western singer Dwight Yoakam. It was a very brief affair – one of several that ran up to her 'engagement' to Bill Macdonald; the romance, that is. It began with her saying: 'I've found a real man and he's sweet and gentle too.' To the next quote: 'I dated Dwight for about six or seven weeks, but that was that. I don't know why anybody wants to make much of it. It was just a short relationship. It was such an unimportant relationship.'

But it was a controversial one after she compared the singer who has a penchant for big cowboy hats to 'a dirt sandwich'. Yoakum, who was thirty-five in 1992, when he was dating Stone, was famous for his skintight jeans and 28-inch waist. 'I don't smoke, drink or eat red meat,' he always explains as his workout routine. He has also admitted to trying to drive a pick-up truck through a girlfriend's house because 'she betrayed our relationship'.

But Yoakum had dated Sharon Stone. What a career move! She said: 'We went on a few absolutely not intriguing dates. People thought it was important because he had that big hat.'

Stone was suddenly everywhere. Actor Richard Grieco was so taken with her *Basic Instinct* performance that, at a film premiere party, he marched up to her and said: 'I've just got to get together with you!' He handed her his telephone number but Stone just looked him up and down and said: 'I'm out of your league, cowboy.' With that, she ripped up his business card and flipped the pieces in the air. Grieco, one of the great young studs of Hollywood in 1993, moped off and didn't even notice other women trying to find his business card and put it, and his contact numbers, back together.

Sharon Stone was rather more intrigued by Chris Peters. Which was probably more to do with antecedents than the lad's 'toy-boy' good looks. She'll never tell now. Peters had some of the best connections in town. His father is Jon Peters and his mother is Lesley Anne Warren, known most memorably for her Oscar-nominated role in Blake Edwards' *Victor, Victoria* in 1982. Peters was an aspiring musician and twenty-four when Stone got involved with him in 1992–1993. She said then, when asked about their romance: 'I like a man who will treat me like a girl. I'm very old fashioned. I *do* wear underwear. Occasionally.'

She had a basic instinct for younger men. Chris Peters' father was a hairdresser who turned himself into a multi-millionaire at the age of twenty-one, before he became involved with Barbra Streisand. With Streisand, he made movies like the third remake of *A Star is Born* and then, with his partner Peter Guber, became the co-production executive at Sony Pictures. Peters was a really big deal. And now his son was dating the hottest movie star in the world. Stone met Peters at a film screening after she had ended her relationship with Dwight Yoakum. As well as being a musician, he had also appeared in films like *The Lost Boys* with, ironically, Stone's movie role rival Julia Roberts' lover, Kiefer Sutherland and Jason Patric. Peters said: 'She was a real fun lady to be with. I think it's better to be a little discreet. But she was fun. She knew how to enjoy herself, how to have a good time.'

He used the past tense, for finally Stone decided: 'We had a beautiful relationship. It was important and real. But I'm too old for him. I have to grow up, get married and have a family.'

Coincidentally, or not, her decision to split up with Peters happened after an incident involving her younger sister Alison. The trio had gone to see *Alien 3*, but when Sharon Stone emerged from the lobby ladies' room she found her sister giving Chris Peters a shoulder rub.

'Hey, what's going on,' she roared in mock horror, adding: 'We may be family but he belongs to me.' She swung Peters around, dipped him towards the ground and planted a smacker of a kiss on him.

That was off-duty fun. Fully establishing herself as a Hollywood power with a chance of longevity was the serious business.

16

Star Control

'Other people, for most of my life, have preferred me
not to think'

– Sharon Stone, 1993

Sharon Stone's friends say that at the time of *Sliver* this apparently ballsy – as Robert Evans had said – actress was not
totally confident, but felt that if anyone was going to mess up,
she would. She wanted some control of her own career – of
her own product. She was now a star and highly marketable.
She still felt exploited by Verhoeven on *Basic Instinct* and had
her friend Mimi Craven on the film set for all the sex scenes in
Sliver.

She had begun seeking control when she believed that *Total
Recall* was going to be a huge success. She fired her agent
Paula Wagner at Creative Artists Agency (CAA), who had
ignored a preview screening of *Total Recall*. Another of
Wagner's clients was Tom Cruise, and Stone says: 'She wasn't
very interested in me.' She went to the Gersh Agency and
says she told them: 'I am thirty-two and I don't want to be
forty-two and not have had a chance.' But as soon as *Basic
Instinct* took off, she sacked the Gersh Agency. She sees
nothing disloyal about it: 'It was simple good business. My
career went from a little mom-and-pop business to a huge
international corporation. I needed people who had international corporate access of their own, as well as enormous
library departments, because I wanted the opportunity to

develop projects for myself. Besides, I didn't have a job. I did have a mortgage.' She went to one of the best agents in town, Guy McElwaine of International Creative Management.

When Robert Evans first announced *Sliver*, he said it was 'going to break down barriers, test new grounds. It's going to examine the fantasy no one wants to talk about – the secret fantasy of voyeurism. All kinds of voyeurism. The picture's not only focused on sex but other sorts, from the most domestic, to the most sexual, to the most heartbreaking.'

And they would include Stone, as lonely book editor Carly Norris, masturbating in a bathtub.

This was a more vulnerable character for her and that didn't help the tensions on the set. She says that for the first time in her career: 'I got serious. Verhoeven dealt with me as an intellectual and forced me to use my mind. Other people, for most of my life, have preferred me not to think, to just shut up, do my hair, stand over there and look good. And could you do it in a bathing suit?

'It's a very male-dominated business, moviemaking, so it behoves me to behave from the male side of my personality, playing by men's rules to do men's work. And then when I go back to acting I can be whole in my femininity. But I'm sort of in a new canoe and I think I am going off in my own direction. And when you take your own path there are more risks involved. So much of making it is just having the guts to stand there until it happens. It's a contest of wills because it's not like anybody is going: "Oh, I hope everything fabulous happens for you!"

'Women have always been the victims in this world. We're trained, from an early age, to submit to men and to bury our integrity beneath this veneer of femininity and stereotyped images of how we should behave. Seduction is a trap. I've played the game for many years because I believed I didn't really have a choice – it's the way the film industry works. But now, I find it more effective simply to be assertive and defend myself as intensely as any man. The key is having no fear.

'All the failed relationships and lousy roles leave you empty inside and you run away from it all. That's why, no matter what happens to me now [1993], I have the mentality of a survivor who has seen where the bottom lies and has no intention of returning to that space.'

Absolutely no intention.

She was now involved very seriously with Bill Macdonald, and the two of them were turning up at public gatherings cooing and hand-holding and cuddling like teenage sweet-hearts. But suddenly, different Sharon Stones appeared for work on the film. There was the real nice lady who bought Christmas lunch for all the cast and crew and staged entertainment with a gospel choir and the internationally famous Cirque du Soleil troupe. Then there was the bravado person-ality who boasted that 'it takes a while for me to calm the men down on love-scene days.' And then the cautious actress who wanted reassurances about camera angles and technical details before leaving her trailer to film the sex sequences.

She and Noyce had battles. One day she accused him of not having a love scene prepared. He says his 'plan' was to per-suade her to provide her own. 'She's as courageous an actor as I've ever worked with – and as good. You're crazy if you don't let an actor take as much responsibility for the story as they can. Sharon has lived Carly's experiences several times over. Only a fool would not consult her.' Or at least listen to her.

But she was touchy. Relations between her and Billy Baldwin worsened when he accidentally stepped on her foot, injuring it. Robert Evans tried to patch things up between his screen lovers. He asked Stone in for a chat, but, instead of helping things, enraged Stone with his story of how Ava Gardner used her sex appeal to control him during the filming of *The Sun Also Rises*. Nevertheless, the kid who stayed in that picture reports: 'Every close-up she did was great. A switch just goes on, lights go on. Selfish, maybe. She's no walk in the park. Charm? Like a barracuda. I wouldn't want to live with her, but I'd sure as hell want to work with her again.'

Maybe not Billy Baldwin. The young actor had attacked *Basic Instinct* for its portrayal of 'lipstick lesbians'. She laughs: 'He may be the lesbian. I mean, Billy's so *young*. I come from Pennsylvania where guys are just sort of regular. No bullshit. They're the guy, you're the girl. In Hollywood, it seems to me the lines are a lot fuzzier. I like most people I have worked with in the business. My vote's out on Billy. I never really quite got his trip. He played a character who was very weird but I never got up to speed on his deal, like whether he was "I am in character" or "I am out of character".'

Evans and his director had other problems than the feud between their two stars; the main one involved Baldwin's penis. Long before *Sliver* began filming in October 1992, the word in Hollywood was that it would involve full-frontal male nudity. But Baldwin's contract allowed him only to be shown naked from the back. 'There isn't a leading man who will do full frontal nudity,' said Evans, with a cynical and less than accurate addition: 'And there isn't a leading lady who won't.'

Baldwin's privates were snipped. The other problem for Noyce, who, by contract, had to turn in a film which the censors wouldn't give the box-office downer rating of NC-17, was the voyeuristic video montage. You could still see about a dozen male private parts, as well as simulated sex, building residents taking showers, masturbation and a couple of sex orgies.

Crew members say Stone and Bill Macdonald would watch the other actors and extras simulate sex, taking showers and dancing around naked. One said: 'Sharon seemed to be really fascinated. One time, she turned to Bill and said: "That looks like fun – why don't we do it?"'

The sex scenes were filmed on a set which the crew members called 'The Passion Pit'. Baldwin, as the skyrise owner, spies on all his residents with hidden cameras. 'There were two almost identical sets at Paramount where all the action would take place. Stage 14 was Sharon's apartment, but 15 was "The Passion Pit". All day long, gorgeous young actors and actresses would act the sex scenes that the Baldwin character would be watching and filming with his hidden cameras. And the wilder and raunchier they got, the more the producers liked it. One that got really out of hand was a strip poker game. Not only did they strip, but these actors grabbed these naked girls and started rolling about on the floor with them. On the floor, on the table, on the couch. In the mornings it was all professional but, by the twentieth sex scene of the day, cast members and crew would be wandering in and out. There was a video monitor set up outside "The Passion Pit" and by the afternoon no one was paying any attention. But it wasn't for posterity. Phillip Noyce took out his scissors . . .'

Snip, snip, snip . . . and finally the radically cropped movie was given an R-rating in America. But getting there had been tough. Tom Berenger and British actress Polly Walker were asked to return to the film for a sado-masochistic sequence. Berenger blew his top: 'That sounds like your perversion,' he yelled at Noyce, adding: 'You can't keep doing these things. I'm not here as a slave. You tricked me into things. I'm holding you to this contract.' Noyce was forced to use doubles.

'Tom is a complete gas,' says Sharon Stone. 'A seasoned professional. Once during rehearsal, when I was moaning: "Tom, I don't know what to do", he said: "You're a soldier of the cinema, march on!" He's a good, old-fashioned guy, happily married, kids. Regular, you know. I like regular.'

And her *Sliver* character was nearer to home: 'Carly is much closer to my personality. That was frightening. It left me feeling a lot more exposed, more vulnerable. I could sense that I was slipping out of her without even realising it.'

For the masturbation scene she wanted to be at her least vulnerable as an actress – to get it accurate, rather than create a male fantasy. 'The first way it was presented to me by Joe Eszterhas and Phillip was as this whole guy thing. About the way guys are when they are by themselves. They wanted me to be looking at a picture of a man in a Calvin Klein "Obsession" advertisement. And I went: "Women aren't like this. For women, masturbation is primarily not a sex thing, it's a different thing. It's a loneliness thing. It's a needy thing. It's a sad thing, a tender thing. It isn't about a magazine or a photograph or a video. Women are not visually motivated in this way."

'I was playing someone fragile, damaged, vulnerable, insecure about sex. Phillip provided space where I could try stuff, let this honest female behaviour be filmed. He was mind-bogglingly supportive.'

There were five women present at the filming of the masturbation sequence, including Mimi Craven. 'They all watched the playbacks and were so happy. It sounds self-serving or obnoxious to say it, but in many ways I felt like they were grateful to see this demonstration of something with a reality-based female sexuality in it. It was a risky thing to do.

'But I do believe it is a very big part of the artist's struggle, to push the parameters of our perception and awareness and those of others. I may not be doing a great job at it but I'm certainly trying to blaze a trail . . . It's strange, but even though *Basic Instinct* had its limits as a work of entertainment, I think it has changed the perception of women in film . . . Audiences are looking for a higher level in interaction between men and women at every level: psychological, sexual, political. The important thing about Catherine was that she was the controller of her own destiny. She toyed with men because they were so wrapped up in their own pricks they couldn't figure her out. She'd have loved to have met her equal. So would most women.'

With *Sliver* she feels she advanced further: 'The sex scenes are very unusual because they let the truth of how some women feel about sex, privately and with a partner, really be seen. It didn't become an exhibitionistic sort of male fantasy of what a moment like that means to a woman. I suppose something so sexually direct, yet so non-exhibitionistic, is going to unsettle people, but you know how it is with sexuality. My mom said it best when she said that the most shocking thing about *Basic Instinct* was that people were more concerned whether or not I was homosexual, than whether or not I was a serial killer.'

But she'd learned her own lessons since The Flash. She was literally covering her ass: 'I had a rider in my contract for *Sliver* that every frame of anything that's nude or partially nude or sexual in any way I get to see and approve of, or it can't go into the picture.'

It was another step on the power-game ladder, of taking control. 'It was a nice feeling. No more cheap remarks and the condescending attitudes of casting agents and directors who think you are just a piece of meat who can be replaced by the next Hollywood blonde thing waiting in line.'

17

The Price
of Fame

'I get followed'
– Sharon Stone, 1993

She's now a mob attraction at the Cannes Film Festival, where she was a 1994 judge. She could not believe her welcome there after *Basic Instinct* and, almost still in disbelief, says: 'People follow me.'

She's been chased down streets in Los Angeles. One fan broke into her hotel room and stole her lipstick. One man, whom police described as a 'sex pest', she discovered lurking at the back of her house. He had cut a hole in one of her rubbish bins so he could hide in there and spy on her.

There were nicer moments. A European billionaire land developer offered her $10 million if she'd marry him, saying: 'You'll never have to work again.' But, of course, that's what she'd been working *for*.

While doing a French *Vogue* fashion shoot on the balcony of the Ritz Hotel in Paris, wearing a low-cut, high-slit turquoise gown, she stopped the traffic in the streets below. She and Mimi Craven work out regularly with personal trainer Paul Gagnon. She does a one-mile incline on the treadmill, then fills in with lunges, squats, leg-lifts and work with some light weights. She's been asked so often for diet advice that she just zips it off: 'Yeah, don't eat sandpaper.'

When she was in a Los Angeles supermarket when it was

being robbed, she was confronted by the gunman. 'He threatened to blow my brains out if I screamed. I stood there waiting for someone to divert his attention. When he looked away, I rolled down the aisle, ran out and called the police. They arrested him but I didn't stick around – I don't want him looking for me when he comes out of the slammer.' The robbery incident in May 1993 just increased her celebrity. Only six weeks earlier, she had filmed television commercials for Pirelli tyres in Europe. They were created by the advertising agency Young and Rubicam, and in them she plays a movie star who lands in a private plane and notices that the tyres in the chauffeured car waiting for her are Pirelli. She becomes impatient with the handsome chauffeur's sedate driving and lures him into the back seat. She then jumps into the driver's seat and takes off for a joyride. She was paid more than $1 million for the commercial. At the same time, she agreed to host the Scientific and Technical Awards at the 1993 Oscars.

She's got the star routine down pretty well. Now. Early in the fame game, she and Mimi Craven arrived at Los Angeles and a limousine met them. They were travelling using their own names, which is a celebrity no-no she now accepts: 'I was so exhausted, I got in the car while Mimi went with the driver to get the luggage, and suddenly a flashbulb goes off and this guy jumps in the car. Horrifying. This idiot was in the front of the limo, leaning over the seat with this huge camera. And he's flashing and flashing and I'm totally freaked out because I just didn't know what to do. And I'm screaming: "Oh, my God, there's somebody in my car!" Which quickly reduces me to screaming: "Get this asshole out of my car!" At which point, Mimi heard my voice and dived through the door at this guy. And I went: "Oh, no, he's gonna kill her." I mean this guy was completely insane or he wouldn't have been in my car. So I grabbed her and kind of wrestled her to the ground. And we were piled on top of each other, hunkering down against this guy . . . And then for months we were certain that the photographs were going to be printed and distorted into some horrifying and perverse tale. We would sneak through those airport magazine racks, looking at the tabloids for our "Lesbian Love Tryst" photos.

'This weirdness is so not my world that, at first, I got myself in some real jams by not knowing the rules. I've had to completely change the way I travel. I thought I could go alone to the supermarket or the gas station, but I know now that I can't do that. I wear a hat to disguise myself.' To emphasise her point, she tells the story of her trip with Bill Macdonald to attend the Italian television awards in Milan.

'I had a point car with two bodyguards, a tail car with two more, and I'm in the middle car with Bill. We think we're covered until a crowd spots us . . . They rip off the rearview mirrors, the bumpers and they cover the car until it's pitch-black inside. They're rocking it, banging it and screaming and I'm thinking: "What if the windows break? What are they going to do to us?" Finally, two hundred riot police had to form a human chain to get us out. What you have to do to keep your sanity is to think the person they want is in another pair of shoes and you're sitting back, wondering what's going to happen to that person. You have to separate yourself. In the car that night we started singing. I figured if we sang we'd be able to keep ourselves together.

'I have to straighten out my karma. I've become a sex symbol which is an absurd thing for me. Particularly, as I symbolise a kind of sex I don't believe in.' However, this is a wily businesswoman and she says: 'Believe me, if people say: "We want to pay you X million to do this movie", I won't be the girl who hangs back saying: "Oh, really, I don't deserve it."'

One side of her fame is something she never imagined: she's regarded by many as a sex expert: 'People ask me all kinds of questions about this kind of stuff and I want to give the most compassionate answers that I can. I don't know why sex has to be such a horrifying mystery. It is really personal. There are so many other natural functions, from a woman's menstrual cycle, to whether or not you feel constipated. And yet you can find answers and relief about that on television.'

By the spring of 1993 she was an icon. Her fame was such that her fans believed she knew everything – and they could ask her anything. She was voted a contender in the 'Favourite Dramatic Actress' category for the popular American 'People's Choice Awards' (she didn't win). She appeared as an auctioneer for the Pediatric AIDS Foundation, selling off a Ferrari 348 Spider for $185,000 – getting $10,000 extra by offering to go for a drive with the buyer, cinema chain owner Paul Goldenberg. He said: 'I kept her to the offer and she kept her side of the bargain. It was great fun – we had a good time. She said the Spider was the only thing faster than she is.'

She happily admitted she was finally cashing-in on making it. For German *Vogue* she did a sensational layout of pictures. She posed with her hands cupping her bare breasts, cigar jauntily stuck in her mouth and what appeared to be a prosthetic penis in her white Giorgio Armani men's shorts. She finished off her outfit with black Oxford shoes and black knee-socks. '*Sie ist das Sex Symbol*' read the headline. And who could disagree? You could debate the taste, but Sharon Stone was the world's blonde.

But, despite all the celebrity, what was going to be her next movie? After *Basic Instinct*, there was a film at Paramount from *Cheers* creators Les and Glen Charles. She could have approval of her leading man. It didn't work out.

There was a drama Michelle Pfeiffer took, opposite Jack Nicholson, entitled *Wolf*, and Rene Russo played Clint Eastwood's love interest in 1993's hugely admired thriller *In the Line of Fire*. Stone explained: 'I got a firm offer to make *In the Line of Fire* with Clint Eastwood who is divine, but there was nothing to the part. I told them it would be cool if they wanted to change the villain [the 1994 Oscar-nominated John Malkovich] to a villainess, but the truth is the script as it existed was perfect.

'I met Mike Nichols [director of *The Graduate, Working Girl* and one of the most admired of American film-makers] on *Wolf* when it was about a man who so disliked people he became a wolf, so he didn't have to deal with them anymore. And he had this veterinarian girlfriend. Then I read another version of the script that had lost its source of humour, where she was sort of a weird hippie kind of chick.

'I never felt that "the projects" came along after *Basic Instinct*. Still, I just decided to go back to work. It came down to: "Look, you are going to do so many projects, some of them will be good and some of them won't."'

Sliver didn't work but it made a fortune. She admits: 'Working on *Sliver* was hell. It was like swimming upstream in an ice-floe. It was creatively a disaster, but it made more than $100 million overseas.' Clever girl. Think of the bottom line – the money.

After *Sliver*, she and her manager Chuck Binder, along with Guy McElwaine, began to map out a long-term career for Stone. She didn't want to take her knickers off ever again, and joked: 'My butt's fallen four inches but my mind is elevated.' But she meant it. And everyone around her knew she did.

Unlike stars of the past such as Marilyn Monroe, who were tied by studio system contracts, Sharon Stone could go her own way. She knew it took a great deal of guts – and talent. Chuck Binder said: 'Sharon always says you can do whatever you want, as long as you don't have fear.'

But she had her turf to protect. She was the new shocking blonde on the block. And then Madonna announced she was going to make a film about a woman who was a sexual deviant and serial killer. Asked about her first reaction, Stone said: 'I'm like: "Go ahead – make my day! I can't wait. I want to be at the premiere. I'm going to sing in the lobby."'

That began a feud between the two which Stone says she regrets: 'I used to think: "Gee I wish we could be friends." And I could call her up on the phone and say: "This is what's happening, can you tell me what to do?" But for some reason we were pitted against each other to the point where she actually bought into it. So I can't ask her questions, although I'd like to because I think she, more than anyone, must know what this is like.

'I went to a party in Beverly Hills and the Press just started to mob me and I was so tired that I wouldn't stop for them to do their whole picture thing. They were really insulted. Then when I came out, they yelled at me: "We're not going to take your picture – you're not Madonna." I thought: "Thank God – at last they know. Why do people keep putting us in the same sentence?"'

There are, of course, similarities. Here are two smart-talking, bad-talking, ambitious women who you feel would simply die if they weren't noticed. Both of them have hurled themselves at celebrity.

But Stone was a success at the movies – something Madonna has never been. That's the basis of the feud. Stone knows that, but chooses to be careful. Madonna's *Body of Evidence* was a bad joke, with preview audiences chortling at her love scenes with Willem Dafoe. Stone said, in remarks which offended Madonna: 'I believe she could act if she got training. The thing is, if you really look at the big picture that girl is not that empty and still doing that much. So I think she's got a barrelful of mystery.

'But the reason I don't think I'm the Madonna of acting is that I think Madonna is a brilliant performance artist . . . She seems to have only one agenda which is to shock. Yet once you shock everyone so much, the shock value is flattened. I'm not looking for one thing to do like that. The one thing I am clear about is that I am a *woman*. And the one thing that I'm clear that has happened is that women are relating to something about me. The makes me feel responsible to be honest about my womanhood.'

What about Julia Roberts? 'I wouldn't want to be Julia Roberts, an enormous movie star when I was twenty-one. I liked being twenty-one. I liked not showing up for my modelling job and staying in bed because I'd gone out all night. Nobody said: "She's a drug addict, she couldn't show up for work." They just said: "Oh, she's twenty-one." Julia Roberts is a young girl. I know what it costs to be where I am, so I'm not going to do anything weird to undermine it.'

18

Media Moll

'I knew from the first minute I met him that I completely understood him and he completely understood me'

– Sharon Stone on Bill Macdonald

Sharon Stone and Bill Macdonald were living together in Los Angeles, and she said they hoped to marry by the end of 1993. That was in the summer of 1993. She was wearing a 1930s Tiffany engagement ring that had belonged to Macdonald's grandmother.

Life had changed since *Sliver*. For a lot of people. When *Sliver* began production, Stone was still seeing Chris Peters. Macdonald was newly married to Naomi Baca and Joe Eszterhas was approaching his twenty-fifth wedding anniversary with wife Geri. By February of 1993, all the couples had uncoupled.

In March of that year, Stone, on an Oscar-night talk-show, announced that she and Macdonald were engaged, despite Macdonald's marital status. 'We love each other very much and are committed to spending the rest of our lives together. My life is full of joy. I'm in love and I'm really happy about it.'

It all seemed so rosy. On the Barbara Walters pre-recorded show on ABC TV – which in Hollywood is seen directly after the Oscar ceremonies – Stone shone like a 1940s glamorous star, wearing lounging pajamas created by Vera Wang. Earlier, she had played her role at the Academy Award ceremonies – it was a triumph for her and designer Vera Wang. Army

Archerd, the official celebrity greeter, said: 'Lots of actresses should simply get help. Extreme decolletage is not appropriate. It's not tasteful and half the audience is looking down the star's dress just from the camera angle anyway. Don't they want people to see their faces?'

Stone – with one billion viewers watching worldwide – had the best of help. Vera Wang put Stone in what she calls her 'blonde dress'. It was simple, elegant and classic, a champagne-coloured duchess silk and satin dress with halter straps. It gave Stone new cachet in Tinseltown – by not being the usual tinsel. Ms Wang said: 'I like a certain minimalism, but with the Oscars you need a bigger silhouette – there has to be a scale to it. So, I put a train on Sharon's dress. You're playing to a room of a monstrous size so the dress needs a certain drama.'

Fred Hayman, fashion consultant to the Oscars and the dean of Beverly Hills fashion, said: 'Her image at the Oscars changed her image as an actress. Everyone's watching.'

Acid-tongued Mr Blackwell, creator of the annual Ten Worst Dressed List, gave his verdict: 'She looked beautiful at the Academy Awards. I thought Sharon Stone was almost the rebirth of the beginning of Grace Kelly. I loved her.'

And so did Bill Macdonald. He was besotted. So, it seemed, was Stone, saying: 'He's a square. Square, square, square! I love it. He's really macho with a deep voice. It gives me such a thrill that he's so square after all these really hip guys with their waist-length hair and their really mellow artistic temperaments. Give me my macho old-fashioned man who says "come here" and I do. The point is, he can take charge and I like that. At this point in my life no one is going to take control of me. The point is finding someone over whom I don't have complete control.'

She talked about sex with Macdonald: 'Sex as a sensual, loving communication is a very interesting thing to me – but every five seconds. That would be too intense to cope with. Real loving – fabulous, generous, intimate sexuality – is not something you want to have every five seconds. I'm over the other thing. I grew out of that.'

So, gone were the toy-boys and the affairs. Here was a real man: 'I knew from the first minute I met him that I completely understood him and he completely understood me. So we avoided each other like the plague until that was no longer possible.'

It was all heartbreak for Macdonald's estranged wife Naomi. She wailed: 'Sharon gets what Sharon wants. I think she's heartless. Welcome to my nightmare.'

It was the start of a media nightmare for Sharon Stone; one she should have expected. Having been turned into the decade's blonde, the image-makers were about to turn on her. She got dumped upon for everything. Front-page news in America was that she had used a real estate agent's home for a photographic session and masqueraded the place as her own. She was seen lounging by the back garden swimming-pool in *Hello!* magazine which proclaimed: 'Sharon Stone photographed for the first time ever in her beautiful Los Angeles home. She's bought her dream home.'

And America's *People* magazine bought the pictures – and the story that the Malibu house belonged to Stone. It is, in fact, the home of commercial real estate broker David Thind, who had met Stone through her manager Chuck Binder.

Thind explained: 'I put the house on the market for $4.5 million and Sharon came to see it. She had a tremendous interest in it. Then she asked if she could use my house for a photo shoot. She said she was embarrassed to use her house and wanted to use mine as representing hers, because they wanted a real show place. I didn't have a problem with her using my house. I gave her permission, but she went a bit overboard.'

In Britain's *Hello!*, Stone was seen photographed by Richard McLaren wearing six different outfits, with captions reading: 'Sharon lives alone in the sunny house filled with natural wood and fabrics. She bought and decorated a beautiful house in Los Angeles.' *People* magazine called it 'a palatial home in the Hollywood Hills.' The reality was that Stone still lived in a one-bedroom, 1,200 square foot house in the Hollywood Hills – on the suburban San Fernando Valley side of those glamorous hills.

It all was niggle, niggle, niggle. Stone's friends say she was having a difficult time coping with the intense media spotlight. Publicly, she said she didn't mind the attention if she was out being 'huh' – her Sharon Stone star persona – but objected to the constant inquiries into her private life.

Her appearance at the opening of a Planet Hollywood restaurant in Chicago was fine – apart from the fact that her luggage was lost en route from Los Angeles and she had to rush out and buy the appropriate jeans and black T-shirt outfit for her rock 'n' roll evening with Bruce Willis, Sylvester Stallone and Arnold Schwarzenegger, the trio of celebrity investors in the restaurant chain. Bill Macdonald watched his bride-to-be shimmying and shakin' on stage. It got so hot that Willis had to strip down to his plaid shorts before he gave a big wet kiss to Stone while a crowd of 3,500, including Don Johnson and Melanie Griffith, screamed and cheered encouragement.

Sharon Stone loves the spotlight. When it suits her.

She couldn't understand the backlash. Australian actor Paul Hogan calls it 'the poppy factor'. As he sees it, there is a field of poppies and as soon as one pokes its head above the others everyone wants to cut it off. It is a good metaphor for stardom.

Stone the superstar and covergirl, and front-page news, found herself in a nasty domestic mess with Macdonald. Naomi Macdonald had decided not to vanish. She would go on nationwide American television and say that Sharon Stone had stolen her husband and, as a result of the shock from that, she had lost her baby.

'I will never forgive that bimbo for robbing me of my husband and baby. That woman has broken my heart in a thousand pieces. I think what she did was cruel.' Later, Naomi said that she and Macdonald were happy. 'Then he dropped the news which destroyed our marriage. Bill said: "Sharon Stone is in love with me. She went to a psychic who told her we were lovers in a previous life. She's left her boyfriend, she's in love with me and I think I'm in love with her." He said he had not been intimate with her because he did not want to shame me. But I later learned that Bill had been lying and the real reason he hadn't slept with her was that she told him: "You cannot touch me until she or you are out of that house."

'I was devastated. I told him I had worked so hard to get to this point where our dreams were coming together and now he was throwing it all away. Bill just looked at me and said: "I know my timing stinks." He kept saying he was confused and pleaded for time to wrestle with his feelings for Sharon.

'I'm a liberal person. I can understand the attraction a man could have for Sharon Stone, so I agreed to give him time. I was determined to show Bill what we had meant to each other. He had been my best friend, lover, husband, soulmate. I did not want to play the clinging, desperate woman. So I made Bill his favourite dinner and we went for a moonlight walk on the beach. We danced to our favourite "Grateful Dead" tape. That night we made love as beautifully as we had ever done. But it was the last time we slept together.'

The next day she flew to Ohio to visit her parents and when she arrived nearly collapsed. 'I thought I was having some physical disturbances because of the emotional strain. I saw the doctor and he said: "No, you're five weeks pregnant." The doctor told me not to get worked up about it, but how could I stay calm after what had happened? We had always wanted lots of babies. I thought this could put the nightmare behind us and we could get on with our lives.

'But when I got back to Los Angeles I knew Bill had slept with Sharon. It was just obvious to a woman that he had not been home. I called him in his car and asked when he was coming home. When he came to the house I told him I was pregnant. A look of horror crossed his face. Then he picked up the phone and called that woman. I could hear snatches of conversation. I heard him tell her I was pregnant. On one of the calls he made that night she shouted at him: "Why does she have to talk to you about this? Doesn't she have any friends she can call?"'

As the drama was played out at the Macdonald's home in Marina del Rey, on the outskirts of Los Angeles, Bill Macdonald and Sharon Stone exchanged more than a dozen phone calls, according to Naomi Macdonald. 'After one call, he said to me: "You can have the baby if you want it, but it might be best to have an abortion." I knew I loved this man and that I was pregnant and that someone was pulling him away from me. I couldn't have an abortion. I'm a Catholic. I was married in the heart of Rome. I loved this man. I would have loved this baby. Thankfully, I wasn't forced to make the decision.'

Macdonald pointed at his wife's stomach and said: 'I am destroying two lives. I am also destroying myself. I'm probably destroying my career for a woman who probably doesn't care about me.'

Naomi Macdonald went to her brother Jerry's house in the San Fernando Valley the next day. It was there that she miscarried: 'I was undernourished, exhausted and had endured something I never thought I could endure. I could barely carry myself let alone a baby. My brother took me to a clinic and it was all over. I couldn't believe it was only five months since Bill and I had exchanged vows in Rome.

'The trauma of losing my husband caused me to lose my baby too. Sharon gets what Sharon wants . . . I know the way this was executed and that's a perfect word. It's like an execution. It was cold-blooded and heartless. I don't know what happened. One day my husband is here with me and the next he's moved out and talking marriage with Sharon Stone.'

It was during the filming of *Sliver* that the Macdonald/

Stone romance became serious, according to someone involved with the film. 'Bill just couldn't resist Sharon's flirting. It went on day after day. They tried to keep it secret, but eventually everyone on the movie knew they were having an affair. Then, with Joe Eszterhas taking up with Bill Macdonald's wife, it's weird. Make a good soap opera though.' If a little unbelievable.

As Sharon Stone's image was being chipped away at, Naomi Macdonald brought out the big chisel: 'Bill told me: "Sharon is worried that she'll look like a homewrecker. So if the Press asks, tell them you didn't like the Hollywood life and left." I decided to tell the truth.'

And then Bill Macdonald's mother Jane got into the action: 'Dump that slut Sharon Stone and go back to your loving wife,' roared one American tabloid headline.

Jane Macdonald lives in a small apartment in Ojai, California, inland from Santa Barbara. She said: 'Sharon's a slut and I hope she doesn't give my son AIDS. I can't believe he'd dump his wife for Slut Stone who talks about all the men she's taken in and thrown out like dirty linen. She's a bad person. For all the things she's done, she could be carrying AIDS. When I talked to him I told him how let down I felt and all he said was: "I hear you loud and clear, Mom." That slut must weave some incredible magic.'

Macdonald and his bride-to-be did not appear publicly affected by this trawl through the media of the rights or wrongs of their relationship. They showed up together at many functions, including a tribute to Michael Douglas who was honoured at the Moving Picture Ball in Beverly Hills in October 1993, where he collected the American Cinematheque Award. At the time, in Hollywood, the word started that maybe this marriage was not going to happen. One problem was money – not Sharon Stone's, but Macdonald's. Unknown to anyone, he had left the Robert Evans Company six months before *Sliver* was released. In August 1993, Macdonald had taken off on an 'Around the World in Eighty Days' style tour, but back in Los Angeles, investigators were looking into his financial affairs. To avoid publicity which might have hurt *Sliver*'s box-office, Macdonald had not cleared his desk until after the film was released.

Evans and Macdonald had fallen out over a movie invest-ment scheme. Macdonald was the head of Axiom Entertainment Incorporated and two other companies, Robert Evans Presents and the Robert Evans Company Incorporated. They were aimed at raising money to produce movies. Legal documents filed in Los Angeles Superior Court show charges against Macdonald that he squandered 'over $5 million raised from Axiom investors in less than six months.'

Macdonald was alleged to have solicited investors from an office at Paramount Studios, offering investors a 40 per cent profit on their money. The lawsuit filed in Los Angeles claimed Macdonald was 'part of a deliberate scheme to defraud investors'. It was alleged that money was siphoned off through kickbacks and consulting fees for work that was never done.

'Bill Macdonald is a slick scam-artist,' said lawyer Mike Inman who, in May 1993, had filed the lawsuit on behalf of seven thousand investors who wanted to 'participate in the production of motion pictures'. In that same year, Inman sug-gested: 'Sharon Stone may be marrying a criminal facing three to seven years in jail.' Later, he said the complex case was expected to be in the Californian court system 'for some long time'.

Apparently more distressing for Macdonald was that, although his annulment from Naomi was completed by December 1993, he and Stone had still not got married. And then there was all the gossip from Vancouver . . .

19

Indiscretions?

'I've really had to grow as a person not to come out of this bitter and scarred'
— Sharon Stone, January 1994

Sharon Stone and her advisers had decided to go all out for a change of image after *Sliver*, and she chased the movie *Intersection*. The leading man was Richard Gere and the director Mark Rydell, who had helmed the Oscar-heavy *On Golden Pond*, which was Henry Fonda's last movie and co-starred his daughter Jane and Katharine Hepburn in 1981. Rydell admits he never even thought of Stone for a role in his movie. But she proved why she is a star. She persisted. After more than a dozen phone calls, he agreed to see her.

At the meeting she was wearing her diamond Tiffany engagement ring on her left hand and her heart-shaped, diamond-encircled-by-emeralds six-month-anniversary engagement ring on her right hand. Rydell presumed Stone was after the role of the homewrecking journalist Olivia Marshak who tears apart the lives of Gere's architect Vincent Eastwood and his prim and prissy but loving wife Sally. Eastwood can't decide between the two women. Should he stay married? Should he leave home and desert his wife and young daughter? Rydell had been seduced by Stone's image. In the opening sequence of *Intersection*, Vincent Eastman is seen in bed with his naked girlfriend. Stone, right? Wrong.

'I was offered the part of the mistress. In fact, I was offered it and offered it and offered it. But I dogged Mark Rydell. I wrote him. I called him, until he finally let me read for the part of the wife. We did it on a Saturday morning. I read with Richard. I did two scenes. Mark told me what I was going to do and then he asked me to do the scene impromtu, where the husband tells the wife he's leaving her for another woman.

'And I decided: "What the fuck? I might as well let her rip."'

'I was stunned,' says Rydell. I expected a moderately talented piece of work. I didn't know the range she has . . . We had her read four scenes and then we threw her a curve. We asked her to read the scene where she has to collapse, when her husband tells her he's leaving her. To see her come apart at the seams was remarkable.

'She pursued this part so avidly she was like a schnauzer on my pant leg. It's a Grace Kelly kind of role and she was so anxious she begged for the opportunity to spend a Saturday with Richard and myself. She was not to be denied. I'm crazy about her. The chemistry between Richard and Sharon was like Gable and Lombard – rich and sexy. She has a more profound acting talent than anyone realises. I respect her as a talent and not as an object.'

Based on the French novel that director Claude Sautet turned into his 1970 film *Les Choses de la Vie*, this version was not a 'vehicle' for any of the players, who included statuesque Lolita Davidovich who made a dazzling debut co-starring with Paul Newman in *Blaze* in 1988. Stone says: 'I'd had my shot at being a sex bomb. It was someone else's turn. I've done that and I've outgrown it. And Lolita was lucky because her part wasn't just a caricature.' For Sharon Stone it was a chance to move on.

Her hair pinned back 'to within an inch of her life', she was the cold, jilted character. It produced another Hollywood controversy about Sharon Stone. The film was scheduled to be released in America in December 1993, but the opening was delayed until the New Year. It was said that Paramount Studio executives did not think audiences would take to a 'cool' Sharon Stone. Rydell said: 'At first, Paramount was trying to make me rush to put the picture out for Christmas of 1993, because they felt it had the star power of Richard Gere and Sharon Stone, which they needed for a big Christmas film. But they finished up conceding to my pressure. The film needed some finishing touches.'

The critics worldwide were divided. But one thing was agreed – Sharon Stone could play Grace Kelly. She could play cool and sexy even with her hair in a bun and not flailing and cascading around.

In Britain the controversial Julie Burchill writing in the *Sunday Times* was captivated by Stone and her performance in *Intersection*. She wrote in June, 1994: 'After seeing this film even her very name seems fraught with meaning, like in Lolita (Nabokov, not Davidovich). Sharon – that terminally working class blue-collar slur – teamed with a surname that blunts scissors and knives and pens! That alliteration, so perfect.

'If Marilyn Monroe spelt Mmmm, and Brigitte Bardot spelt bébé, then Sharon Stone spells Ssss, a hiss with a kiss, a cobra with a cause. She is where babe meets barbarian

'She is quite, quite magnificent.

'Stone here is more beautiful than she ever was, moving slowly in neutrals and pearls towards the garishness of Davidovich but if you'd never seen her before you'd never know she was famous for sex. The one sex scene she plays – in flashback, as a young married woman in her father's house, coerced by her husband, fully clothed, on top, on tenterhooks – is a masterpiece by itself; funny, tragic and totally original. And shocking in a way that her skin stuff never was.

'Stone stalks through her scenes with seamless, supple skill which even Pfeiffer couldn't crown; an utterly fresh take on the injured party girl, so betrayed that she's half drunk on it and half bored with it. Her presence evokes a shoal of screen legends – Greer Garson, Alexis Smith, Tippi Hedren,

Catherine Deneuve – while spinning on the sharp end of her own unique brilliance.

'When she's on screen the film looks like a classic you'll remember forever. Stone's role is relatively small but she cuts through the whole film and in the end rescues it.

'Stone's performance is one of those scary, shimmering things that keeps people going, against all odds, to the cinema. She is an actor of such rare and uncouth talent that she makes all those women we *thought* we loved – Geena Davis, Meg Ryan – look rather mannered and twee.

'We fell asleep with Catherine Tramell; we woke up with Sharon Stone. Right now, it's hard to think of anything better.'

The 'serious' critical raves were appreciated. But, publicly, the sexy Sharon image would not go away. Bill Macdonald had spent much time in Vancouver on the set of *Intersection*, and workers on the film said Stone was leading him around like a lovesick puppy. He carried her purse. He was always there to light her cigarettes. Richard Gere invited Macdonald for 'a night out with the boys', but Stone intervened with a snappy: 'He has other plans.'

Bill Macdonald found himself, the one-time macho square man in control, now cast in the role of wimp. And Sharon Stone found Frank Anderson, a Canadian stockbroker. Anderson, 6ft 5ins tall, is a financial wizard, certainly tall, and dark and handsome as well. Stone was in her limousine, driving through Vancouver, when she spotted Anderson in his Ferrari. The window of the limousine whirred down. They started talking at a traffic light.

'They saw each other while Sharon was making *Intersection*,' said someone working on the film. 'They kept it pretty quiet and usually met at a cabin in the woods outside of town. It's a romantic hideaway owned by Frank's boss, Harry Mall. Frank said that what was important was that word of the affair didn't get around, because Sharon wants to keep it under wraps. He'd told me it would cause a lot of problems if it leaked.'

It 'leaked'. Like a sieve. Anderson could not hide his pleasure at being involved with Stone. He talked about it with friends.

His boss and friend Harry Mall was with him on a business trip to Los Angeles and they stayed at the Peninsula Hotel in Beverly Hills. Their plan was to have dinner there with Stone and some Japanese investors . . . but plans changed location. Anderson took Stone with him when he met the Japanese businessmen at his boardroom in Vancouver. A business associate said: 'Frank can't help showing her off when they go to restaurants. When the Japanese saw Frank standing in the boardroom with Sharon Stone it disrupted everything. They couldn't believe it. He's already got a big reputation as a playboy and doesn't need to prove anything to anyone – including Sharon.'

Anderson himself was disdainful of inquiries. In Vancouver, sources said that was because Sharon Stone didn't have to prove anything to him. It was an *Intersection* – as in a 'holiday' – romance. She left town and it was all over. Everywhere.

From July 1993, Hollywood believed Macdonald was being led along by Stone, but constantly she or a spokesperson would say it wasn't so. Marriage, babies, happiness very soon were the idea. Rumours also persisted that she was involved with Revlon cosmetics billionaire Ron Perelman. By January 1994, it was being said that 'Sharon dumped Bill because she couldn't deal with the fact that nothing much was going on with his career.'

Sharon Stone defended her side of the situation in an interview in January 1994, when she said: 'I never went on a date with Bill. We talked on the phone. I told him he'd have to change his life if he wanted to see me. Which he did. We plan on getting married. I'd love to have a family. It was a bizarre episode to have my life turned into a media event, to be painted to look like something I'm not was very hurtful . . . Yet, in a strange way, it was like a spiritual renaissance for me, because I've really had to grow as a person not to come out of this bitter and scarred.

'I never expected such a public addressing of private matters. Why people should think this is news I'm really not sure. Because these kinds of things occur every fifty-seven seconds and nobody cares . . . And I don't believe that my existence in this area is any more valuable than anybody else's. I don't know what the big deal is.

'We love each other very much and are committed to spending the rest of our lives together. Primarily, I feel and think how happy I am to have found such a beautiful love in my life and how grateful I am for the existence of that love.'

Flash-forward to April 1994 and Sharon Stone is saying: 'Bob Wagner is my current love interest. He is not married. He is a very talented young man with a great sense of humour and I love being with him. He has not moved in with me permanently.' That was an official announcement through Stone's publicity people.

Unofficially, Stone had told Macdonald it was over before she began work on the 1994 film *The Quick and the Dead* – her 'Clint Eastwood Western'.

Westerns rode back into Hollywood on the back of Kevin Costner's *Dances With Wolves* and Clint Eastwood's Oscar-sweeping *Unforgiven*. Stone was clever enough to see the trend and decided that she should co-produce a Western with herself as the starring protagonist. In 1992, Carolco had planned to pay the then number one movie lady Julia Roberts $7 million for the same sort of adventure movie, called *The Revengers*. Sharon Stone was now getting the same sort of money plus percentage profit 'points'.

The Quick and the Dead was backed by the Sony Corporation's TriStar Pictures – the distributors of *Basic Instinct*. Stone was working with people she knew. It was anticipated as one of the major blockbuster films of 1994–1995. Stone saw that instantly and went into her control mode.

British moviemaker and screenwriter Simon Moore's script for *The Quick and the Dead* began being offered for sale in Hollywood in 1993. Moore, who wrote and directed the English thriller *Under Suspicion* which starred Liam Neeson (who became a major power player in 1994 as the star of Steven Spielberg's *Schindler's List* and the UK television series *Traffick*) wanted to make the film himself. That is, produce and direct it. But, as we now know, Sharon gets what she wants. And pays for it.

One million dollars to Moore.

After she had read the script about a tough Wild West woman out to revenge the death of her father, a story packed with a motley assortment of characters with names like Fly, Flatnose, Ratsy, Ace, Kid and Herod – our heroine's opposition – she couldn't resist.

Sharon Stone, who had waited all these years for stardom, was literally going to blow away the opposition. She couldn't get over the thought of being a bang-bang John Wayne/Clint Eastwood type, but she could see the commercial and career value. She was headin' up and movin' on. Again.

Simon Moore wanted to direct his screenplay. But Stone wanted the former music-video maker Sam Raimi, who had so chillingly led *Darkman* and *Army of Darkness* for the big screen. She had studied; she knew what she wanted. She got the script, the vehicle literally to ride on from *Basic Instinct* and she wanted Raimi. The only hurdle was Moore, who was based in North London.

Sharon Stone says: 'I was adamant about Sam making this movie. I got to the point in the production where I was fighting for everything. People say I'm a pain in the neck but that's OK. Having a reputation as a bitch makes people stay back a little bit. I don't mind it that much.

'*Sliver* was my big learning experience. I had the right to say no to all kind of things in my contract so that I rolled over in an effort not to be difficult, to be a good girl. And everything I rolled over on became the enormous errors of the picture. So I got to the point in the production of *The Quick and the Dead* of fighting for everything. "I am not rolling over on this. It will not be less than this. It will go like this." I became very adamant that the quality of the piece be maintained.

'By the time we were ready to make the movie I didn't want to make it – I was so worn out. The night before the read-through of the script I was running a 102 degree fever because I didn't want to face going. But by the time I left the rehearsal I was all right. We did all the fighting before we got to Arizona.

'Sam was the only person on my list. It's the kind of picture I don't think just anyone could have made, even great directors, because of the kind of material it is.'

'When Sharon Stone says: "I want you", what man could feel bad?' asks Sam Raimi.

Although he had never worked with 'name' actors like Stone and Hackman before, he was not concerned about being intimidated. What did worry him was directing a Western comprised mostly of gunfights: 'I was a little scared at first. There's a fine line between the cliché of previous Westerns and the classic aspects of previous Westerns. Is the gunfight something that's so cliché the audience really doesn't want to see it anymore? Or is it a classic element that has gone beyond the cliché and into the myth of the thing? We wanted to bring a new edge in.'

Simon Moore was paid more than $1 million not to direct. 'He's very happy,' is all that his agent would say in February 1994. And he should have been. Sharon Stone was in the Arizona desert, dealing with the horrid hot days, the chilling nights, her conscience about Bill Macdonald and her interest in the then twenty-seven-year-old Bob Wagner.

The movie, in which she co-stars with Gene Hackman – the Best Supporting Actor Oscar winner in 1993 for Eastwood's instantly classic Western *Unforgiven* – as the real nasty of nasties, was being filmed about fifty miles from Tucson, Arizona.

After she met Wagner, Stone telephoned Macdonald and told him he no longer had an 'open' invitation to the white-painted adobe home she had rented in Tucson. Then he got an even more mind-blowing call: 'Miss Stone will be sending your ring back by Federal Express.' There was no mention of the other ring, the 'anniversary' one with the diamonds and emeralds and everything, and none of the people involved will talk about it.

On the set of *The Quick and the Dead*, Sharon Stone and Bob Wagner were very much a couple. One of his jobs was to go to her trailer, tell her she was needed for filming and give her technical details. One of his first jobs on the film was simply to pick up Stone at 5.30 a.m. each day and take her to the film location. One time they were late, and the production people had to send out a team to find them.

But that was no problem. Sharon Stone was the boss on the film-set in Mescal, Arizona, which was doubling as the town of Redemption where she had to go up against Gene Hackman's villain Herod in a deadly gunfighting competition.

'Do we have any blood around?' asks actor Kevin Conway on the film location. He is looking up from a mud-pit at Sharon Stone who is in full 'High Range Drifter' gear, sodden Stetson, spurs and long, frocked riding coat, and holding a pistol to his head. The make-up man dashes over to Conway, playing Eugene Dred, the brothelmaster of Redemption. As a red liquid is being poured into Conway/Dred's lap, Stone smiles and tells him: 'Your penis has been shot off!'

The rain is pouring down on the mud-pit and Stone looks over to director Sam Raimi and asks: 'Should I kick the gun away? That's the way Angie Dickinson would do it.'

Angie Dickinson as Sergeant Pepper Anderson on television's *Policewoman* was a breakthrough for women's place in action roles in the 1970s. Sharon Stone was moving it along for the 1990s. When they saw the first footage from the film, film executives said they thought that Stone could possibly wear Old West women's clothes. 'Some people who shall remain nameless wanted me to wear a dress to ride into town. I thought: "Oh yeah, the gunslinger's going to ride into town *side*saddle." There's a stereotype to everything . . . I was so darned mad. And there were some people who shall also remain nameless who were concerned that there really weren't a lot of places for me to be naked in this movie. But there are a lot of ways to be sexy other than flouncing around in your birthday suit. This character's not trying to run around in the nude so she can get control over somebody.'

But that didn't mean there would not be nudity and sexy moments in *The Quick and the Dead*. This was frontier feminism – Sharon Stone style. 'It was a pleasure, for every day I went to work we would experiment with what it would be like to be trapped in a situation in the Old West. And because I didn't have to fit into some agreement of femaleness I got to be really female.

'In the old movies they made them wear those unbelievably stupid hairdos like, excuse me, where did they get the cream rinse and curling iron? The whole depiction of women in film has been a joke. It's rarely a picture of a woman as women really are. It's more a man's perspective, a man's fantasy of a woman, than the way women actually do anything. I go to the movies with my girlfriends and we come out of the picture going: "Do you do that? I don't do that."'

Before her gunfight with the brothelmaster, Stone spent seven days covered in mud. She wore a diver's wet suit under her cowgirl/gunslinger costume and plastic bags on her feet to keep out the wet. 'She's very unglamorous in this movie and she's the one who wanted that,' said Judianna Makovsky. She found much of the wardrobe used in *The Quick and the Dead* in a vault in Milan. They were the original costumes from the Sergio Leone/Clint Eastwood Westerns, authentically aged.

Stone is not always unglamorous in the movie. Ms

Makovsky explained: 'Of course, the studio wanted her to look good, and we certainly didn't want to pretend that she wasn't feminine. The leather pants helped with that.'

Stone found any debate about her femininity amusing: 'Well, you know, I think we've pretty permanently established my gender, I think that's an element we don't have to view as a mystery anymore.'

But there is mystery in *The Quick and the Dead* – and fear and evil. Redemption is a chilling town with a Satanic-looking house at one end of the main street. Behind it there is only blistering hot, high desert. Inside lives Herod. Hackman, in mutton-chop whiskers and bowler hat, plays him as a Beau Brummell. A deadly dandy.

'I thought about predatory birds when I designed Herod's house,' said production designer Patricia Von Brandenstein, adding: 'And about Dickens, because this is a place where bad is very bad, good is very good, and, in the end, people get what they deserve. This is a town in which there is no commerce, no society, no school and no sheriff. Children don't thrive here and babies aren't born. But now a cleansing rain has hit Redemption. It's all very allegorical, but it's not tongue-in-cheek.'

All the gunfights were choreographed like a ballet, all different movement and style. As well as Hackman – in reality the man with the fastest gun in Hollywood – veteran Western stars Pat Hingle and Woody Strode appear in the action.

For the younger audiences, Russel Crowe (who played a skinhead in the 1993 film *Romper Stomper*) and Leonardo DiCaprio (who starred as the retarded boy in 1994's *What's Eating Gilbert Grape?*) appear. They are the youngsters in the life – and bed – of Stone's gunslinger, slapping an altogether different sort of leather from gun holsters.

But the bullets fly. 'I just love the violence,' says Stone, her Colt Peacemaker on her hip. 'Whenever somebody suggests cutting it back, I'm like, *no*, more violent. I want it to be *more* violent. There's something about a period movie, and particularly a movie that's this kind of new genre, that takes the reality out of the violence, it doesn't romanticise it.'

As co-producer of the film (with famed director Stanley Donen's son, Josh), she attended to every detail, including getting her brother Michael a role as a nasty in the movie. She also took Michael as her 'date' to the 1994 Oscars. Gossips went crazy trying to identify the man with the slicked-back hair and long ponytail who seemed perfectly at ease with the screen's sex goddess. Sharon Stone, transformed after the ceremonies in a flapper-fashion beaded dress pulled sharply down over her left shoulder and with her hair crimped 1920s style, was constantly asked to introduce her new hunk.

She did it with delight. She has always kept close to her family, but most of all to her parents and brother. Her two sisters have always been kept in the background. Sharon Stone will not discuss why.

Michael Stone isn't a pretty picture like his sister. His nose has been broken several times and he spent two years in New York's Attica prison for possessing a kilo of cocaine. Michael Stone, who was forty-two in 1994, said: 'I was a marijuana smuggler in the 1970s and then just got swept into the major league. With me, smoking a joint was small in comparison to being totally whacked out of your mind on alcohol. I was in the Air Force after graduating from school and after I got out I began dealing drugs. I guess I was trying to buy my way out of the working class. I resented the fact that my father spent his whole life working in the steel shop. I thought I could beat the system.'

He followed his sister to Hollywood and started a marble and stone business and became involved with Rona Newton-John – Olivia Newton-John's sister. In 1994, they had been together for six years.

'Had it not been for Sharon and my parents I probably would still be in jail.'

He shut down his marble and stone business in 1993 – he

had helped decorate many celebrity properties, including producer Aaron Spelling's $20 million mansion – because of the recession. Meanwhile, he had been studying acting. Sharon Stone suggested him for *The Quick and the Dead*. She laughs: 'They were like: "OK we've got to see her brother." But they kept putting it off until the bigger parts were cast and then my brother came in and they said: "Oh he's fabulous!" I was so happy about it. He's a good, natural actor.' Michael Stone did not have one line to say in the film. But he is beside Gene Hackman for most of the movie.

And Sharon Stone was in almost every frame of celluloid, which is also the case in *The Specialist*. Stone took one week off to look after her interests in Los Angeles after *The Quick and the Dead* completed filming in February 1994. Then she went to Miami to co-star with Sylvester Stallone in *The Specialist*, which was directed by cult favourite, Peruvian Luis Llosa.

The movie was made completely on location in Miami and Miami Beach. Stallone (being paid $12 million) was a retired US Government explosives expert with a secret. Stone (taking home $6 million dollars for her role in 1994's big action movie) was the beautiful sultry woman bent on revenge. The plot involved a family of mobsters and a renegade killer for hire, and Warner Brothers touted the film as 'a sensual suspense thriller of vengeance, obsession and betrayal.'

Involved in the action were veteran actor Rod Steiger, James Woods and Eric Roberts – brother of Julia Roberts. In Hollywood it is a *small* world.

'This is a dream,' said Stallone. 'This movie hinged on getting the perfect leading lady and that's what we got.' He would say that, wouldn't he? But in Miami the crew – always the sharp-end of information on any film – said Stone was the perfect femme fatale.

However, not all the crew were allowed to be present when Stone and Stallone shot some *Basic Instinct*-style sex scenes. Only three cameramen and two technicians – out of a film crew of 212 – were allowed behind the locked doors. They all had to sign confidentiality agreements before the three days of steamy filming began. It wasn't Stone who was suddenly shy, but Stallone.

Apparently, he had a 'thing' about his bouncing bottom being on public display in reality, rather than on film. 'He definitely had a thing about his butt,' said one of the crew, adding: 'He figured the guys would trade a few stories around the bars if he humped Sharon in full view of everyone. So he had the director film it behind closed doors.'

The love scenes were filmed in a shower, on the floor of an apartment and finally, more conventionally, in bed. 'I've never seen anything so erotic, so sensual or so sexy in my life,' said the movie's producer, mogul Jerry Weintraub. He added: 'Stallone reminded me of a young Jean-Paul Belmondo, while Sharon was everything she was in *Basic Instinct*.'

For Stallone *The Specialist* was an altogether different action movie. 'The Italian Stallion' they named him after *Rocky* which, of course, was a boxing movie. So, what would be the next title for the resurrected box-office champion following his encounter with Sharon Stone? 'Lucky'?

The Specialist was filmed mainly in the South Beach area of Miami – Hollywood on the Atlantic – and attracted more paparazzi than Stallone's regular entourage of bodyguards, hairdressers, stylists and drivers. And that's a lot of Nikon. There were long lens shots of Stallone in action but the photographers concentrated mostly on Sharon Stone. Especially on the day she wore a see-through pearl/mesh dress with only the briefest white bikini briefs to allow some modesty.

'Sharon Stone is a big asset,' says Stallone, who calls their first encounter in the film 'an erotic explosion'.

There was no screen rivalry between them, he says, but those on the set said there could have been some contest over who could wear the tiniest bikini briefs. The winner? Stone, they suggested, finally succeeded.

At 47, Stallone looked remarkable during filming in May in 1994. The body was bronzed by the Florida sun and so toned that just by smiling the muscles rippled. Rocky and Rambo were never conventional sex symbols but rather powerful action heroes. Romance was always a count of ten or bursts of frenetic firepower away.

With the title role of *The Specialist* he was firing on altogether different cylinders as well: 'This movie is a foray into a genre that I've been longing to do for a long time – an erotic thriller. There's a great deal of difference between an action film and an erotic thriller. Obviously I've kind of digressed at times and gone into comedy and lost audiences when I did it. The comedies I tried didn't work for me. Throughout my career I've tried, I've really tried. I try to take chances and I find there's resistance.

'Usually in everyday situations I consider myself rather humorous. I enjoy the absurd very much. The comedies I've done have not done very well. Either that's my failure or, more importantly, I think that the vehicle itself wasn't suited to my personality. I think comedy is best left to comedians and I'll stick with what I'm doing. I tried and the main thing is I learned from failure. I don't learn from success. I learn from failure.

'Certain actors become like a product and when you go to a movie you expect a certain kind of result. The message I get is: "If I want to see a comedy I'll go and see Steve Martin – I don't want to see *you*. From you I expect something else." And that's always Rocky, Rambo, Cobra. They relate to that. So I said: "To thine own self be true."

'This is what I am – why not make the best of it? I think I do fairly well in this genre. I understand it and I like the danger. I like the challenge. Once you come to terms with something, once you accept what you are, where things are, then there's no conflict.'

In 1993 he enjoyed huge hits with Alpine high jinks in *Cliffhanger* and the futuristic fantasy *Demolition Man*. He had no doubts during filming that *The Specialist* could be his biggest success ever with the box-office combination punch of

Stallone and Stone. They really sizzled to the beat and heat of Miami music and several songs written for the movie by Gloria Estefan. Stallone said: 'I finally dealt with the erotic side of my personality. I played a man who lives in the shadows – he was a mysterious character.

'But the movie was more about this man who leads a voyeuristic life and this relationship he developed with Sharon Stone. He begins to do business with Sharon over the phone. Her family was killed years ago and she wants revenge for that. He doesn't want to work with her because he feels something's wrong but the way she speaks to him on the phone is so seductive. He becomes enamoured and he follows her. He goes into her apartment and sees how she lives. He immerses himself so deeply into her psyche that when he finally meets her it's an erotic explosion.

'For this kind of film Sharon is it – the actress I would most want to act with. She has this genre, this particular mood, covered so I guess I made the right choice. Bette Midler wasn't available so we went with Sharon.'

The last remark, of course, reminds us why Stallone should not do comedy. But he was at his most relaxed. He says the set of *The Specialist* on Miami Beach ('I'm getting paid for this!') had been the smoothest running of his career. 'There's been no difficulties no prima donnas? Sharon? A delight.'

Stallone's mother Jacqui was not so impressed by her son's latest movie partner. On a Toronto television show she was asked about Stallone's lovelife and said: 'I told him to stop running around with those floozie tramps. He's filming a movie with the tramp of the decade, Sharon Stone, and I warned him to stay away from her. My son needs a decent Canadian woman.'

The crew on *The Specialist* had a different view: 'She has guts and grace, which is a terrific combination,' was the report from the Fontainebleau Hilton Hotel and Resort where the moviemakers had set up headquarters. 'Sharon and Sly are clever casting – this is going to be an enormous picture. They both have giant followings and this film has lots of sun, sea and, yes, sex . . . You've got the two top bodies in the same movie. The script is packed with action. This is today's Cary Grant and Grace Kelly. It's *To Catch a Thief*. How can it fail?'

One thinks of Robert Evans . . . but how *could* it fail? *The Specialist* did have the 1990s elements of 1955's *To Catch a Thief*, in which Cary Grant as a reformed cat burglar romances the needs-to-be-warmed-up Grace Kelly. Sharon Stone knew how to play icy blondes. But not how to use a high-powered rifle, despite becoming quite a hand with a revolver in *The Quick and the Dead*. She had to learn that for *The Specialist*. Typically, she worked so hard she became something of a crackshot at target shooting. She challenged Stallone to a match at a range in Florida's Dade County. He won. She asked to make it the best of five. And went back to the shooting range.

Bang, bang, bang. .

Blue Angel?

'I dress up to show that I am happy'
– Sharon Stone, 1994

Sharon Stone was Hollywood's class act. She knew what was wanted and she was delivering. But she also knew the parameters: 'I'm not going to be able to make this kind of money for an extended period. I have a certain archetypal look, but maybe not anymore now that I'm aging.'

Nevertheless, she had become an important person in Hollywood. One of the town's biggest stars. And her appeal was international. In August, 1994, a British marketing survey of moviegoers named her the world's sexiest film star. She could call a tune. Or tunes. And she was no longer regarded as the obligatory beautiful blonde. Martin Scorsese, arguably America's best director and longtime collaborator with Robert DeNiro, persuaded her to work with the two of them on his 1995 film *Casino*. The film, which began filming in Las Vegas in October 1994, focuses on the seamy side of America's gambling capital and was written by Scorsese and his 'Goodfellas' collaborator, Nicholas Pileggi.

But she was not always gracious with her success. She had her own special security guard during the filming of *The Specialist* in Miami, a man who had worked for Richard Nixon's White House. When Nixon died in May, 1994, the

security guard asked Stone for a few days off to attend his former chief's funeral in Yorba Linda, California. Stone told him
if he went he could forget his job. The bodyguard went anyway – and his employment abruptly ended. Stone's publicity
people in Hollywood insist he has 'resigned'.

Such were the hurdles of dealing with fame – and
power.

Asked if she was happy in 1994, she said: 'Real happiness
comes from inside. Nobody can give it to you. I think I am
happiest playing with my god-daughter, happiest when I am
with friends, when I am cooking dinner for friends.'

But there were also book deals. She was wanted as a
celebrity interviewer to talk to people as diverse as the Dalai
Lama and California mass murderer Charles Manson. Stone
also used her celebrity to help homeless children in Los
Angeles. At Camp Unity in the city she would do 'cooktimes'
and help the children bake chocolate chip cookies.

She said: 'I'm not the Michael Bolton of acting', talking
about the widely thought of 'white bread' singer, and adding:
'I take risks. I'm there to inspire some thought or feeling. Now,
the thought or feeling is up to you – the inspiration is up
to me.'

Sharon Stone was a superstar with worries in 1994. Asked
about men, she said: 'I know how to deal with them!'

But what about her future?

'A lot of people think that fame is a Band-Aid that cures
their ills. I'm no kid and I knew long before I became famous
that wasn't the deal. I'm the court jester – not the Queen. But
when you get zipped into movies that can do a lot for a lot of
people.'

Sharon Stone is a superstar. Hear her say: 'There isn't one
tight-bottomed twenty-five-year-old girl I've met who knows
what I know. There's no replacement for life's experience.'

But tight bottoms work in Hollywood.

Oh, really?

In the spring of 1994, Sharon Stone had been made an offer

she could not refuse. Would she portray Marlene Dietrich in a film version of the biography written by the legendary German star's daughter?

Not a problem.

What will the boys in the backroom say?

What Sharon Stone says: 'As long as you don't have fear you can do anything . . .'

She proved her point at the 1995 Cannes Film Festival. There it was revealed that she had signed a $50 million dollar deal with Miramax Films which, in effect, turned her into a Hollywood mogul.

She will either star in or produce – or both – a string of future projects which as well as the Dietrich film include a remake of the 1958 Kim Novak comedy *Bell, Book and Candle*.

Would this mean she was stepping away from her 'Basic Instinct' image? Yes, she thought. And then at a Cannes charity dinner she turned up in a Valentino thigh-high gold silk hot-pants suit. It was a reminder of a stunt played by Madonna in the French resort and Stone said: 'Anything Madonna can do I can do better.'

Hollywood tycoon or not she had not lost the movie star presence. Or her penchant for raunchy movie promotion. The weirdest, wildest and – depending on your point of view – hottest sex scenes of 1995 were in *Casino*. Stone, as the wife of Robert De Niro, has to submit to the sexual demands of that other Scorsese regular Joe Pesci.

'He'll kill her if she doesn't,' explains Stone adding: 'That's why the sex scenes are so charged. I wouldn't call them love scenes.'

Audiences do not see Stone or Pesci naked but she added: 'There is certainly an indication that we are.' Pesci, a foot shorter than Stone, enjoyed his S/M lust encounters. How about his leading lady? 'These scenes are always the easiest to film. But these were certainly *unique*.'

And she plans to keep presenting more sensation. She's

called her company Chaos Productions but Miramax co-chairman Harvey Weinstein expects big profits not disorganisation: 'There's no star around that's more glamorous or smarter. With payments and shares of the profits as star and producer she won't be making peanuts.'

The deal ran full circle in her basic ambition: 'It feels great to be a mogul because when I was a kid growing up in Meadville, Pennsylvania, I said I was going to be an actress and everyone told me I was crazy. It took me thirteen years before I had a hit movie. It took a lot of willpower and fortitude to keep working towards my dreams.

'Now, I want to run the entire movie business.

'I'm in control at last.'

FILMOGRAPHY

Stardust Memories:
United Artists, Jack Rollins, Charles Joffe. USA, 1980.
Director: Woody Allen. Starring: Charlotte Rampling, Jessica
Harper, Marie-Christine Barrault, Tony Roberts, Helen
Hanft, Sharon Stone.

Deadly Blessing:
Polygram, USA, 1981. Director: Wes Craven. Starring: Maren
Jensen, Susan Buckner, Jeff East, Ernest Borgnine, Lisa
Hartman, Lois Nettleton, Sharon Stone.

Irreconcilable Differences:
Lantana/Warner Brothers, USA, 1984. Director: Charles
Shyer. Starring: Ryan O'Neal, Shelley Long, Drew
Barrymore, Sam Wanamaker, Allen Garfield, Sharon Stone.

King Solomon's Mines:
Cannon, USA, 1985. Director: J. Lee-Thompson. Starring:
Richard Chamberlain, Sharon Stone, Herbert Lom, John
Rhys-Davies, Ken Gampu.

Allan Quatermain and the Lost City of Gold:
Cannon, USA, 1986. Director: Gary Nelson. Starring:
Richard Chamberlain, Sharon Stone, James Earl Jones,
Henry Silva, Robert Ronner.

Cold Steel:
Cinetel, USA, 1987. Director: Dorothy Puzo. Starring: Brad
Davis, Sharon Stone, Jonathan Banks.

Police Academy 4:
Warner Brothers, USA, 1987. Director: Jim Drake. Starring:
Steve Guttenberg, G.W. Bailey, Bobcat Goldthwait, Sharon
Stone, Bubba Smith, George Gaynes, Leslie Easterbrook.

Action Jackson:
Silver Pictures Production/Lorimar, USA, 1988. Director:
Craig R. Baxley. Starring: Carl Weathers, Craig T. Nelson,
Sharon Stone.

Above the Law:
Warner Brothers, USA, 1988. Director: Andrew Davis.
Starring: Steven Seagal, Pam Grier, Henry Silva, Sharon
Stone, Daniel Faraldo, Nicholas Kusenko.

Total Recall:
Carolco, USA, 1990. Director: Paul Verhoeven. Starring:
Arnold Schwarzenegger, Rachel Ticotin, Sharon Stone,
Ronny Cox, Michael Ironside, Marshall Bell, Rosemary
Dunsmore.

Year of the Gun:
First Independent, USA, 1991. Director: John Frankenheimer.
Starring: Andrew McCarthy, Valerie Golino, Sharon Stone,
John Pankow, Mattia Sbragia.

He Said, She Said:
Frank Mancusco Junior Productions/Paramount, USA, 1991.
Directors: Ken Kwapis, Marisa Silver. Starring: Kevin Bacon,
Elizabeth Perkins, Sharon Stone.

Scissors:
DDM Film Corporation, USA, 1991. Director: Frank De
Felita. Starring: Steve Railsback, Sharon Stone, Ronny Cox.

Diary of a Hitman:
Continental Film Group/Vision International/Continental,
USA, 1991. Director: Roy London. Starring: Forrest
Whitaker, Sharon Stone, Sherilyn Fenn.

Basic Instinct:
Carolco, USA, 1991. Director: Paul Verhoeven. Starring: Michael Douglas, Sharon Stone, Jeanne Tripplehorn, Leilani Sarelle, George Dzunda, Dorothy Malone.

Where Sleeping Dogs Lie:
Columbia TriStar, USA, 1992. Director: Charles Finch. Starring: Dallas McDermott, Sharon Stone.

Sliver:
Robert Evans Productions, USA, 1993. Director: Phillip Noyce. Starring: Sharon Stone, William Baldwin, Tom Berenger.

Intersection:
Bud Yorkin Productions/Paramount, USA, 1994. Director: Mark Rydell. Starring: Richard Gere, Sharon Stone, Lolita Davidovich, Martin Landau, David Selby, Meaghan Eastman.

The Quick and the Dead:
Columbia-TriStar, USA, 1994. Director: Sam Raimi. Starring: Sharon Stone, Gene Hackman, Leonardo DiCaprio, Russel Crowe, Pat Hingle, Woody Strode, Michael Stone.

The Specialist:
Warner Brothers, USA, 1994. Director: Luis Llosa. Starring: Sylvester Stallone, Sharon Stone, Rod Steiger, James Woods, Eric Roberts.

Casino:
Universal, USA, 1995. Director: Martin Scorsese. Starring: Robert De Niro, Joe Pesci, Sharon Stone, Kevin Pollak, James Woods.

Index